# Acknowledgments

Many organizations offered their support to the development of this book. Heartfelt thanks to (in alphabetical order) Ashford Capital Management, Bombay Hook National Wildlife Refuge, Bowers Beach Maritime Museum, Camden Friends Meetinghouse, Camden Parks Department, Causey Mansion Refresh, Choptank Mill (Dan Draves), Commission on Archives and History of the Peninsula-Delaware Annual Conference of the United Methodist Church, Delaware Academy of Medicine, Delaware Agricultural Museum and Village, Delaware Nature Society, Delaware Public Archives, Delaware Historical & Cultural Affairs, Delaware Historical Society, Delaware Society for the Preservation of Antiquities, Delaware State University (Loockerman Hall), Delaware Tourism Office, DNREC Division of Fish and Wildlife, Duck Creek Historical Society, First State National Historical Park, Friends of Old Dover, Inc., Friends of Old Swedes, Friends of Prince George's Chapel, Friends of the John Dickinson Mansion, Gordon / Fournaris & Mammarella, Greater Harrington Historical Society, Hagley Museum & Library, Historic Odessa Foundation Inc., Kalmar Nyckel Foundation, Lewes Historical Society, Tom Marvel, Milford Historical Society, Milford Museum, National Park Service, Nanticoke Indian Center, New Castle Historical Society, Old Courthouse - Georgetown Historical Society, Old Library Museum (New Castle, DE), Pencader Heritage Museum, Smyrna Museum, St. Jones Center for Estuarine Studies, Ted Harvey Conservation Area, Zwaanendael Museum.

# Preface

The arrival of the railroad marks the clear end of one Delaware era and the beginning of another. Prior to 1832, any of its business owners needing to get a sizable quantity of goods to Philadelphia, the closest major market, were forced to ship them via water.

It was impractical to cross the Delmarva north by land to reach Philadelphia or east to access Maryland ports oriented to Baltimore, the next closest market. The overland route was a dense tangle of marshes and undergrowth, roads were narrow and unreliable, and no wagon could compete with a ship for the amount of available cargo space. These realities shaped where towns arose along the Delaware Bay, how well they thrived, and what industries dominated.

The appearance of the New Castle & French Town Railroad in the early 19th century hurled Delaware society towards a complete re-orientation from sea to land travel.

If one looks hard enough, traces of the early Delaware maritime era can be seen all around. Modern development has taken longer to reach the Delmarva peninsula, largely cut off from the mainland until the Chesapeake Bay Bridge was built.

Consequently, Delaware's stock of colonial structures has for the most part remained undisturbed far longer than many other colonial era states. Its key historical sites are more readily accessible today. This book attempts to show the reader as much, with current photographs. They trace Delaware history from 1638-1832. This period encompasses the first Swedish explorers setting foot on this peninsula's shores, to the appearance of the first railroad.

Tucked in around this time line you'll find sidebars explaining various colonial era traditions such as blacksmithing, clock making, and hunting/fishing/trapping, to name a few.

I hope you enjoy taking this journey as much as I enjoyed assembling it for you.

# Contents

**Pages 56-65**     Delaware ratifies US Constitution, Abolition societies form in Wilmington and Dover, Sussex county seat moves to Georgetown, second Constitutional Convention meets in Dover, Bank of Delaware founded, Wilmington Town Hall built, Yellow fever strikes Wilmington, HMS DeBraak sinks, Dupont builds first gunpowder mill, Commodore MacDonough victorious in War of 1812, British bombard Lewes, state cedes Pea Patch Island to Federal control

**Pages 67-73**     African Union Methodist Protestant church founded, grain merchants become key to Little Creek, steamboat industry launches in Wilmington, Chesapeake & Delaware Canal operations get underway, Lafayette returns to Brandywine, first public schools open

# Accompanying Sidebars

How did Delaware get its name? It begins with a storm at Cape Henlopen and a Virginia navigator who had lost his way. (cont. on pg. 75)

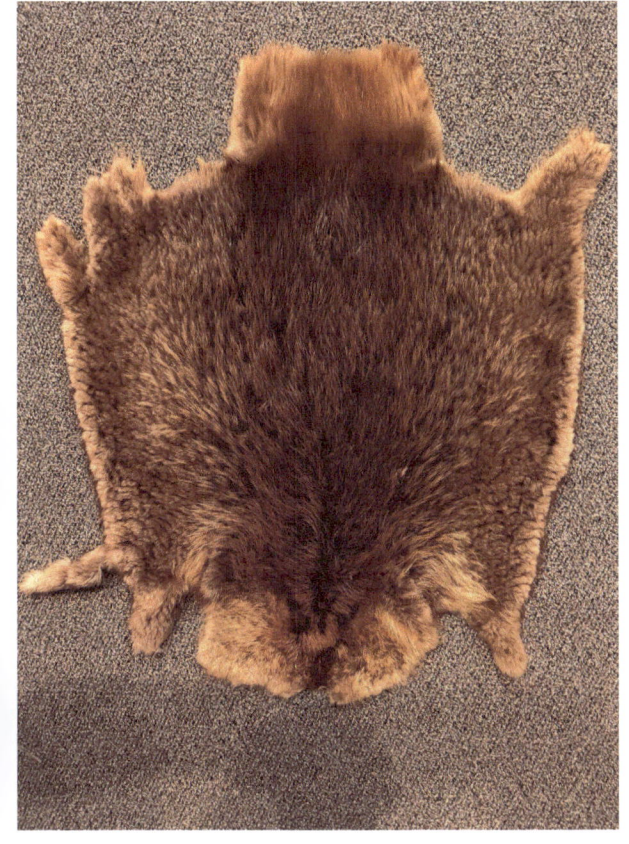

**Above Left:** More than 10,000 years ago, the earliest settlers of Delaware arrive from Asia, emigrating across the Bering Strait. The Lenni Lenape refer to themselves as "the original people," though they in fact share the peninsula with the Nanticokes, Choptanks, Pocomokes, Accomacs, Wiccomiss, Assateagues, and others. But it is the Lenape the Swedish and Dutch traders encounter in 1638. The Europeans want furs, and later maize, and in exchange bring metal goods and fine woven blankets. (cont. on pg. 75)

**Above Right:** Detail of a modern model depicting daily life in a Lenni Lenape village shows a rack of animal furs drying in the sun. (cont. on pg. 75)

What drives the Swedes to establish a colony in North America? New markets for copper.
(cont. on pg. 75)

**Left:** Peter Minuit moors the *Kalmar Nyckel* at a natural outcropping on today's Wilmington riverfront called 'The Rocks,' a point he deems easily defensible, and well sited for beaver pelt trade with the Lenape, and builds a simple fort. (cont. on pg 76)

**Below:** The Europeans initially build crude log cabins, the first of their kind in the New World. (cont. on pg. 76)

## Slavery in Colonial Delaware

Slave labor is critical to the development of early Delaware's plantation economy. Compared to larger colonies, though, there are relatively few slaveholders, smaller scale plantations, and therefore smaller slave units. Early and influential Quaker and Methodist sway pushes the colony towards elimination of the practice. Colonial-era slave quarters are roughly built, as shown by this handhewn beam **(right)**, at a slave cottage on the Parson Thorne mansion grounds in Milford. Few examples of early slave homes exist today, as most were wooden structures allowed to rot and decay over time. This slave domicile at the Causey Mansion **(below)**, also in Milford, is therefore a treasure. A male slave at John Dickinson Mansion in Dover peers out a window **(far right)**. In the early part of the 18th century, both slaves & freedmen attended white churches but were relegated to sitting in the gallery, as at Barratt's Chapel in Frederica **(far lower right)**. (cont. on pg. 76)

**Right:** By 1658 the Dutch have built 100 homes fanning back from the waterfront location of the hotly contested Ft. Casimir (below). The Dutch house whose interior is shown here is built during this period. It still stands today, thanks to the 1937 efforts of the Delaware Society for the Preservation of Antiquities, which rightly recognized its historical value in telling New Castle's Dutch origins. Today, it's maintained by the New Castle Historical Society. (cont. on pg. 77)

**Left:** 1651 - Peter Stuyvesant, Dutch governor of New Netherland, builds Fort Casimir (now New Castle) just a few miles south of Fort Christina on the Delaware. Settlers are quickly installed nearby. Model designed and built by Donald A. Reese and his industrial arts students at William Penn High School in the 1970s. The design is based on the Lindstrom drawing of Fort Trinity (Swedish) of 1654. (cont. on pg. 77)

1659 - Lewes is founded.
(cont. on pg. 77)

**Below:** Francis Whitwell, being given a blank warrant for land in 1674 or 1675 by Capt. Edmund Cantwell of Cantwell's Bridge (Odessa), lays claim to "Land for the Coming att the Water [*sic*]" (Bower's Beach) in St. Jones (now Kent) County. He describes it as "a town which none would Like," "being all sunken," which caused him to build "upon the outermost part a pretty distance" from water's edge. (cont. on pg. 78)

Mouth of St. Jones River empties into Delaware Bay at Bowers Beach.

## Colonial Plantation Life

Kent County's Kingston-upon-Hull **(left)**, patented 1671 by George Wales, is one of the earliest of the state's coastal plantations, situated close to the mouth of the St. Jones River. The English had taken control of the colony from the Dutch only 7 years prior, which may help explain why this tract was named after a British town. Corn, tobacco, wheat, and hay are key export crops. It would be generations before the rich virgin soil became depleted due to lack of fertilizer use and no crop rotation.

The typical plantation is surrounded by a cluster of outbuildings: a smoke-house **(right**, from the Buena Vista Mansion in New Castle), wood shed, granary, ice-house, and more. (cont. on pg. 78)

Immanuel Church founded 1689, New Castle.
(cont. on pg. 78)

**1688- Dover Courthouse removes to "James Maxwell's Ordinary, site of Dover."**
(cont. on pg. 79)

The "hundred" is an administrative subdivision dating back to Colonial times.

HUNDREDS: Delaware is the only state that uses the English term 'hundreds' to delineate a division of a county. In 1682 William Penn directs that the lower three counties of Pennsylvania be divided into townships made up of 100 units (there is much debate, even today, among historians whether Penn's intent was every hundred families, every hundred farms, or even every hundred men capable of bearing arms). These townships are referred to in an April 9, 1690 order from the Provincial Council as 'hundreds' and have been called that since. Penn starts with 12 hundreds; today there are 33, including a "Little Creek Hundred" in both Sussex and Kent Counties.

1698- Holy Trinity - Old Swedes Church - is built in Wilmington. Shown here and bottom left. (cont. on pg. 79)

**Collins-Sharp House (ca. 1700)
is today one of the early extant
homes in Odessa.** (cont. on pg. 79)

1698-1700: Pirates, including Captain William Kidd, maraud along the Delaware. Kitts Hummock, shown here, gets its name from him. Pirates commandeer Pilot boats to board their target ships. (cont. on pg. 79)

OOTH

**Left:** In 1704 the "three lower counties" of Pennsylvania (New Castle, Kent & Sussex) secede from the colony's other counties after a long series of disagreements with the rest. (cont. on pg. 80)

**Right:** The Green, in Dover, formally laid out in 1717, is meant as a gathering place for the towns-folk. William Penn sites Kent county's courthouse and Assembly chambers to face it. (cont. on pg. 80)

![Swedish plank house interior]

**Swedish plank house, built late 1700s, Smyrna (restored)**

**Above:** This little single-story plank house has been preserved as one of the last original examples of early Swedish Delaware plank dwelling architecture from the late 1700s. (cont. pg. 81)

**Right:** Short's Landing is one of the earliest river stops to serve the new town of Duck Creek Crossroads (today Smyrna), followed inland along Duck Creek by Hay Point Landing, Rothwell's Landing, and finally Smyrna Landing. (cont. on pg. 81)

**Short's Landing along Duck Creek (restored)**

**Below:** The Kent County side of Milford is first settled in 1680 by Henry Bowan on what is known as the Saw Mill Range. A century later, the Reverend Sydenham Thorne builds a dam across the Mispillion River to generate power for his gristmill and sawmill. Around the same time, Joseph Oliver lays out the first city streets and plots nearby on a part of his plantation. Soon, a number of homes and businesses appear along Front Street and Milford is born. (cont. on pg. 81)

Parson Thorne Mansion, Milford, built 1730-5

## Colonial Building Details

The Dutch lose control of Delaware to the British in 1664, but Dutch architectural influence continues deep into the Colonial era, as can be seen on this entry to Brecknock (right), built in Camden in 1740. Brecknock is not a Dutch word; rather, it's the name of a Welsh shire capital. As is typical of early Dutch houses, there's no pretension to this entryway. There are only one or two steps, as Dutch-style houses are close to the ground. There's a stoop (from the Dutch word 'stoep,' used the way we use it) with 'settles' on either side to give an inviting appearance. The batten door was originally on leather hinges.

Brecknock, Camden, built 1740

Jacob Dingee House, Wilmington, built about 1771

The Jacob Dingee House of Wilmington (left), built about 1771, is a fine example of how Delaware builders emulate the Flemish bond brick pattern popular in Philadelphia at the time. Flemish bond is a decorative bond, one that lends visual quality to a wall surface. The bond's alternating stretchers (sides of brick) and headers (ends of brick) form a pleasingly patterned regularity, requiring skill to execute. The Dingee house uses dark glazed headers on the second floor, shown here, changing to 'common' bond a few courses above the first floor line. The structure is an example of an 18th-century urban residence continually occupied by working families—carpenters, bricklayers, contractors—and is one of the few surviving dwellings of downtown Wilmington's period of Quaker settlement (1736-early 1800s).

Vincent Loockerman and Delaware State University
(cont. on pg. 81)

Delaware's decision to separate from Great Britain and Pennsylvania, as well as the writing and adoption of the first state constitution, takes place at the New Castle Court House in 1776. The building's cupola serves as the beginning point of the 12-mile radius that determines Delaware's curved northern boundary. (cont. on pg. 81)

**New Castle Courthouse seen through a raindrop.**

**Above:** In 1739, Willingtown (recreated here in modern day Wilmington) requests and receives a royal charter. The name is changed to Wilmington. Why the change? As always, politics isn't far from the surface. (cont. on pg. 82)

**Right:** In 1740, William Shipley and partners build Delaware's first sea-worthy vessel, a brigantine christened *The Wilmington,* in the town of the same name. The brig pictured here is a 1740 ship named *Sv Petr Sv Pavel* (St Peter St Paul), for comparison only. No images of *The Wilmington* exist. (cont. on pg. 82)

**Above:** The earliest structure of the First Presbyterian Church in Delaware and the third place of worship in Wilmington. (cont. on pg. 82)

**Right:** Carpenter/cabinetmaker Samuel Canby of Bucks County, PA moves to Wilmington in 1742, bringing his sound business sense along with him. He builds the first flour mill of consequence on the lower Brandywine in 1770, buying up valuable mill property over the next 12 years. Canby's original mill is long gone. However, Walker's Mill, shown here, is near Canby's site. Built 1813-16. (cont. on pg 83)

The Pennsylvania rifle was the perfect hunting firearm of its time. German gunsmiths begin to immigrate to the Lancaster area of Pennsylvania, 71 miles west of Philadelphia, starting in 1709. There, they develop innovative techniques of boring gun barrels that lead to the long rifle, which shoots a ball farther and more accurately than the smoothbore musket. 17th century Dutch settlers had clung tenaciously to older firearms such as the matchlock and the wheel lock, but the English settlers of the new century are more willing to embrace the new Pennsylvania rifle.

Up to about 1850, deer, red foxes, turkeys, woodchucks, ducks, pheasants, rabbits, squirrels, geese and doves hunted thus provide generations of Delawareans with meat for the table.

The first oyster dredges seen in Delaware Bay are those of Connecticut watermen who sail into the area in the early 1800s. The unregulated hauls expand to as much as they please. Delaware notices, and in 1812 passes the first law limiting oystering to Delaware and Maryland vessels and establishing other parameters. Prior to the 19th century, oyster shells are valued for their use in lime mortar for brick buildings, road surfacing material, and, when burned, as an ash fertilizer for the fields.

## Colonial Hunting/
## Trapping/Fishing

Muskrat, opossums and raccoons provide winter meals for the Nanticoke of
lower Delaware, a fishing and trapping
people, long before the arrival of the
European settlers. They and other local
Algonquin tribes add mink, otter and
beaver to their trapping roster when
Swedish and Dutch fur traders seek to
do business. Later settlers trap, like the
Native Americans, both for furs and for
food. The iron spring traps shown here
appear after 1820.

Early Swedish and Dutch settlers must have
been astonished at the odd forms of sea life in
their new colony, many of which had no com-
parable equivalents in the Old World. This lack
of familiarity leads to the circulation of misin-
formation. For example, one Stockholm author,
Thomas Campanius Holm, writes of the newly
discovered "sea spider" (crab) in his History of
New Sweed Land (1702) that they had tails like
edged swords, with which they could saw down
trees.

Model of the USN Sloop of War *Wasp*, stationed in Lewes and active during the War of 1812. (cont. on pg. 83)

**Right:** Docks at Port Mahon harken back to a style that would have been common in Lewes in the late 18th century.

**Far Right:** Replica of the 1767-era Cape Henlopen Lighthouse which now stands in a traffic circle in Rehoboth Beach. (cont. on pg. 83)

**Old Christ Church, Laurel, built 1770-2**

They were called 'chapels of ease' by their parent churches in Wicomico County, MD because they provided a satellite spot to worship for outlying parishioners. Neither Prince George's Chapel in Dagsboro nor Old Christ Church in Laurel became a part of Delaware's religious network until 1791. The Episcopal Church in Delaware codified its formal structure at that time. The two chapels are therefore of interest as an illustration of the long Delaware-Maryland boundary dispute's influence on church affairs. (cont. on pg. 83)

**Prince George's Chapel, Dagsboro. built 1755**

1764 - Charles Mason and Jeremiah Dixon survey Delaware's western boundary. This Mason-Dixon Line marker is at the town of Marydel. (cont. on pg. 84)

**Left:** The pharmaceutical ingredients shown here aren't from any one apothecary's inventory, but represent a cross-section of 18th century compounds. They include benzine, oil of peppermint, and also items we wouldn't today necessarily associate with a druggist's dispensary: saffron, peppercorns, and on the far right, mercury.

**Center:** Compounding and dispensing drugs wasn't the apothecary's only work. They also administered enemas. 'Clyster' syringes were used to administer enemas. Penile syringes treated gonorrhea or syphilis. The British syringe shown in the middle is made of brass. The two American syringes are made of pewter.

**Below:** Amputation in the 18th century was called the Capital Operation. It's easy to see why: it had the largest tools, the largest mortality rate, and in many ways was the most technical surgery a surgeon would perform. This capital saw, used to amputate large bones, is from 1780.

## Colonial Medicine

**Left:** 18th century dental tools include a tooth saw (left) and tools known as 'English keys' (middle and right) for pulling teeth. The sand dollar, almost pure calcium carbonate, is ground and mixed with a binder and other ingredients. The concoction is used both for fillings and the creation of false teeth.

**Center:** A mortar, the symbol of the apothecary, is arguably the oldest of all pharmaceutical equipment.

**Below:** Tools for bloodletting. Early medical practitioners believe there are four main "bodily humors": blood, phlegm, black bile, and yellow bile. They conclude an imbalance in any of these humors creates the need for either bloodletting, purging, or vomiting. Virtually every known medical condition at one time or another is treated by these methods. (cont. on pg. 84)

Printer James Adams sets up his Wilmington shop in 1761. During his first year he announces the publication of a schoolbook, a 'ready reckoner,' the 1762 *Wilmington Almanack* **(below left)** along with a piece called *The Advice of Evan Ellis to his Daughter when at Sea*. The *Kentucke* book, 1784, features one of the first maps of Virginia's then Kentucky County, drawn up by author John Filson in consultation with Colonel Daniel Boone. It is an immediate sensation. In 1776 and 1777 Adams prints Continental currency notes **(below)** for the colonies/newly emerging country. (cont. on pg. 85)

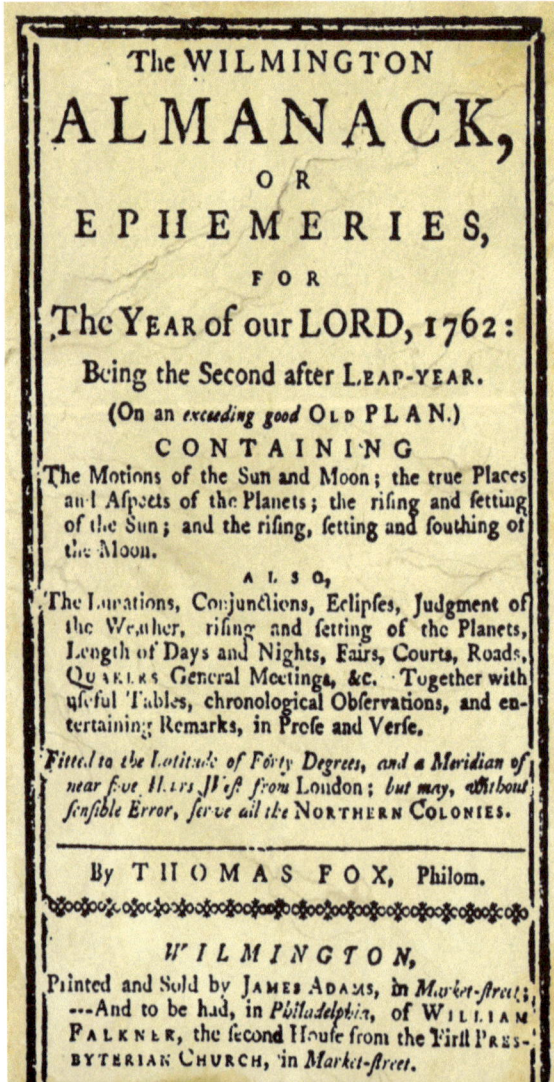

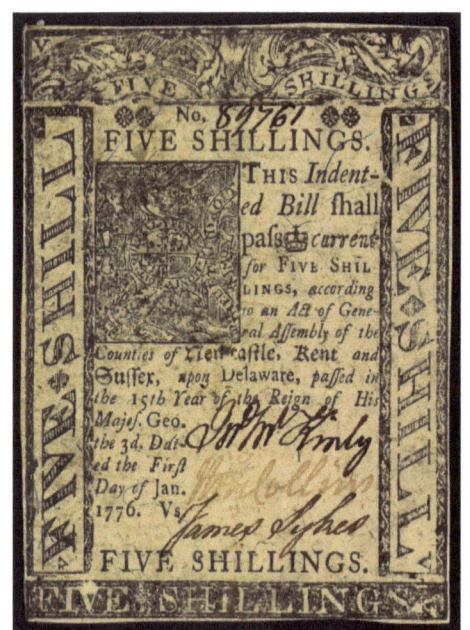

**1765 - Newark Academy, precursor to University of Delaware, moves to Newark.** (cont. on pg. 85)

In 1767, William Corbit opens the first industry in Odessa, a tannery. His success is reflected in his estate. (cont. on pg. 86)

Corbit House
Exterior

# Blacksmithing

In October 1641 the *Kalmar Nyckel* and the *Charitas* bring to New Sweden the first expedition of Swedish (and some Finnish) colonists qualified to create a self-reliant community. A blacksmith is among them. For at least 2-½ centuries after that, the blacksmith is a pillar of any small farming community. Just how crucial is the blacksmith to developing village life? For an answer, look no further than Hockessin. There, the Quaker settlers erected a Friends Meeting House in 1738. By the 1820s, some 80-plus years later, only two other structures serving the public had been built: a school and a blacksmith shop. (cont. on pg. 86)

1767-68 - John Dickinson writes 'Letters from a Farmer in Pennsylvania,' an influential protest against British policies towards the colonies. (cont. on pg. 86)

George Read owned the original house here. Fire destroyed it; his grandson built this dwelling.

The Delaware counties are eager to be represented at the Congress called to meet in Philadelphia in the fall of 1774 (now called the First Continental Congress) to protest the coercive measures adopted by Parliament after the Boston Tea Party. Delaware sends Caesar Rodney, George Read, and Thomas McKean as its delegates. (cont. on pg. 87)

Law office of Thomas McKean at time of the First Continental Congress.

1776 - Caesar Rodney rides horseback all night (July 1-2) from Dover to Philadelphia to vote on resolution for independence. (cont. on pg. 87)

1777 - State Capital moves to Dover.
(cont. on pg. 87)

On December 9, 1775, the Continental Congress resolves that a body of troops be raised in Delaware "for the defense of American liberty." Commanded by Colonel John Haslet, the Delaware Regiment consists of more than 500 battle-ready troops. They march northward to join the Continental Army in August, 1776. (cont. on pg. 88)

The Battle of Cooch's Bridge breaks out near Newark on September 3, 1777, the only Revolutionary War engagement in Delaware. (cont. pg. 88)

George Washington moves troops to an area in the vicinity of the Hale-Byrnes house property in Stanton after Cooch's Bridge and holds at least one meeting there to plan for Philadelphia's defense. (cont. on pg. 88)

The day after defeating George Washington at the Battle of Brandywine, British General Howe sends a troop detachment to Wilmington, then a town of 1,250, and takes possession. This advance guard captures John McKinly, President of Delaware, and confiscates money, plus New Castle County public and private records. The following day the British occupy the town in force with *Roebuck* and *Liverpool* at anchor on the Christina. Many of the local homes are turned into field hospitals for the British. (cont. on pg. 88)

Francis Asbury and Thomas Coke meet in 1784 at Barratt's Chapel in Frederica **(top)**, establishing The Methodist Church as a separate denomination in the US. Old Bethel Church in Lewes (1790) and Barratt's Chapel are the only two 18th century Methodist Preaching Houses to have survived in Delaware to the present day. (cont. on pg. 89)

## Homespun Domestic Clothing

Velvets, satins and silks are found only in the homes of the wealthiest families in Colonial times. For the average household, linen and woolen wear are the mainstays. Fabrics are coarse but serviceable. After the men break and hackle the flax **(lower right)** and shear the sheep, the women do all the subsequent work of carding, spinning, weaving, bleaching and dyeing.

**1756 - Choptank Mills in Marydel is one of the longest running mill businesses in the state...up till 1982. (cont. on pg. 89)**

**1802 - Nathaniel Whiley builds what later becomes Abbott's Mill near Milford; today a museum with still functional equipment.** (cont. on pg. 90)

**1640 - Ashmond Stidham builds first gristmill in Delaware, in Wilmington.** (cont. on pg. 90)

1787 - December 7 - Delaware ratifies the United States Constitution at this Dover tavern and becomes the 1st state in the Union. (cont. on pg. 90)

The GOLDEN FLEECE Tavern

First & Central Presbyterian Church, Wilmington. In 1800, Pastor Francis A. Latta founds and becomes president of the Delaware Society for Promoting Abolition. (cont. on pg. 90)

Warner Mifflin, founder of the Abolitionist Society in Dover (1788), rests in the Motherkill Friends Quaker Burying Ground, Magnolia. (cont. on pg. 90)

**1791 - Sussex county seat moves from Lewes to Georgetown. (cont. on pg. 90)**

(cont. on pg. 90)

An 18th century trial is a public spectacle among the 3 county courthouses in the Delaware colony. Crowds swell to several hundred, and no sergeant-at-arms wishes to yell out results repeatedly. Instead, with a special colored spear in hand, he steps outside the front door and shows the public either the white side—"not guilty"—or the red side—"guilty."

**1792 - 2nd constitutional convention meets.**

Delaware's General Assembly calls for a new constitutional convention in September 1791. The resulting Delaware Constitution is the second guiding document for Delaware's government, supplanting the 1776 original. (cont. on pg. 91)

The state legislature incorporates the Bank of Delaware in early 1795 with a capital stock of $500,000 ($11,758,373 in today's dollars). It is the state's first public bank. (cont. on pg. 91)

**Bank of Delaware 2nd headquarters (1816)**

Wilmington Town Hall bell calls forth the community for 75 years. (cont. on pg. 91)

The first structure in Wilmington created for government use is the Town Hall. The Borough Council requests the building committee design a structure to be "built in a plain and handsome manner." Construction begins in 1798 and is completed the following year. (cont. on pg. 91)

Philadelphia refugees flee a yellow fever outbreak in August 1798. Their arrival in Wilmington causes a town panic. The Wilmington Mercury briefings published by the Board of Health help calm the populace. (cont. on pg. 92)

## The Wilmington Mercury.

Printed Occasionally and Delivered *Gratis*—to the Patrons of The Delaware Gazette—By *Smyth*.

### TUESDAY EVENING—SEPT. 18, 1798.

#### HEALTH-OFFICE.

The great Expence at which the Board of Health procure Nurses and Neceffaries for the Sick at the Hofpital, and the exhaufted ftate of their funds, compel them to call upon their fellow-citizens in town & country, to affift them by Donations. As they are in want of every neceffary of life, it is ufelefs to enumerate the articles—in fhort, there is nothing that can be ufeful at the Hofpital, but will be thankfully received by the Board of Health, at the Health-Office, near the Town-Hall.——And, as they are under the neceffity of making continual advances of cafh, they will thankfully receive for the relief of their fuffering fellow-citizens, any fums which may be put into their hands.
Publifhed by Order of the
Board of Health,
JAMES LEA, jun.
Secretary.
Wilmington,
Sept. 17, 1798.

*Deaths for 24 hours, ending Tuef-day evening—6 o'clock:*
Sarah Hendrickfon,
Rachael Lake,
Haflet Monro,
James (fon of Thos.) Patterfon,

#### DEATHS,
From Auguft 7, to September 18—inclufive.
Adults,     90
Children,   6
    Total,  96
*Remaining in the Hofpital,*
16 perfons—three of whom are dangerous.

*Donations Received fince our laft:*
From Edw. Worrell, five dolls. cafh.
W. C. Smyth, half-a-guinea, do.
John Ferrifs, ten dollars do.
John & Wm. Warner, five gallons port-wine.
Fifteen dollars, cafh, from a citizen.
John Fleming, 15lb. fhell'd barley.
Chriftopher Hollingfworth, 12 lb. fugar.
Sundries bedding, from a lady unknown.
Jofeph Bringhurft, junior, ten gallons vinegar, and 6lb. fugar.
2 bottles fherry wine, and 2 do. port wine.
Jofhua Jackfon, load of ftraw.

*Publifhed by Order of the Board,*
THOMAS MENDENHALL,
President;
JAMES LEA, jun. Secretary.

Duncan Beard

Thomas Crow

## Colonial Clockmaking

Clockmakers Thomas Crow, Christopher Weaver, and Duncan Beard are highly sought after for their exquisite craftsmanship.
(cont. on pg. 92)

Weaver/Duncan

Christopher Weaver

James Drew, British captain of the *HMS De Braak*, had captured a Spanish prize ship, the *Don Francisco Xavier*, which was headed to Cadiz with a South American cargo of cacao beans and copper valued at £160,000 sterling ($3.9 million in today's dollars). Captured ship in tow, Drew meets pilot boats from Lewes a mile offshore on May 25, 1798. Foul weather combined with an extraordinary gust of wind flips and sinks the *De Braak*. Some of the *Xavier* crew swim to safety, but the rest of their mates, Captain Drew, and some prisoners are swiftly pulled under and perish. (cont. on pg. 93)

**1798 - War sloop HMS De Braak sinks off coast of Lewes**

Between 1802 and 1921, the portion of the Brandywine River Valley nestled in Wilmington is the site of one of early America's important and most successful industries - the E.I. duPont de Nemours Powder Co. This gunpowder factory's commercial endeavors launch one of today's giants of the chemical industry. (cont. on pg. 93)

**1802 - DuPont builds first gunpowder mill along the Brandywine.**

**Birthplace of the 'Hero of Lake Champlain'**

Commodore Thomas MacDonough, the 'Hero of Lake Champlain,' outnumbered both in men and ships, captures the entire British fleet in the Battle of Plattsburgh, Sept. 11, 1814. Combined with Matthew Perry's 1813 Lake Erie victory, MacDonough's crushing blow, to everyone's surprise, paralyzes the British invasion of Canada. This house, in the town of Macdonough, is near the 1783 birthplace of the Commodore, who was born in a log cabin on this property. (cont. on pg. 93)

The War of 1812 has a major impact on the town of Lewes. The British naval blockade initiated in March of 1813 lasts for most of the next two years. With maritime commerce limited, the local economy suffers. The regular presence of troops results in the use of many structures in the town for military purposes, and a camp for militia and US Army Regulars is established near Blockhouse Pond. (cont. on pg. 94)

In 1813, during that same war, Delaware cedes Pea Patch Island to the Federal government for the purpose of building a fort. Army engineer Joseph G. Totten designs the first Fort Delaware, shown in his 1815 sketch here. (cont. on pg. 94)

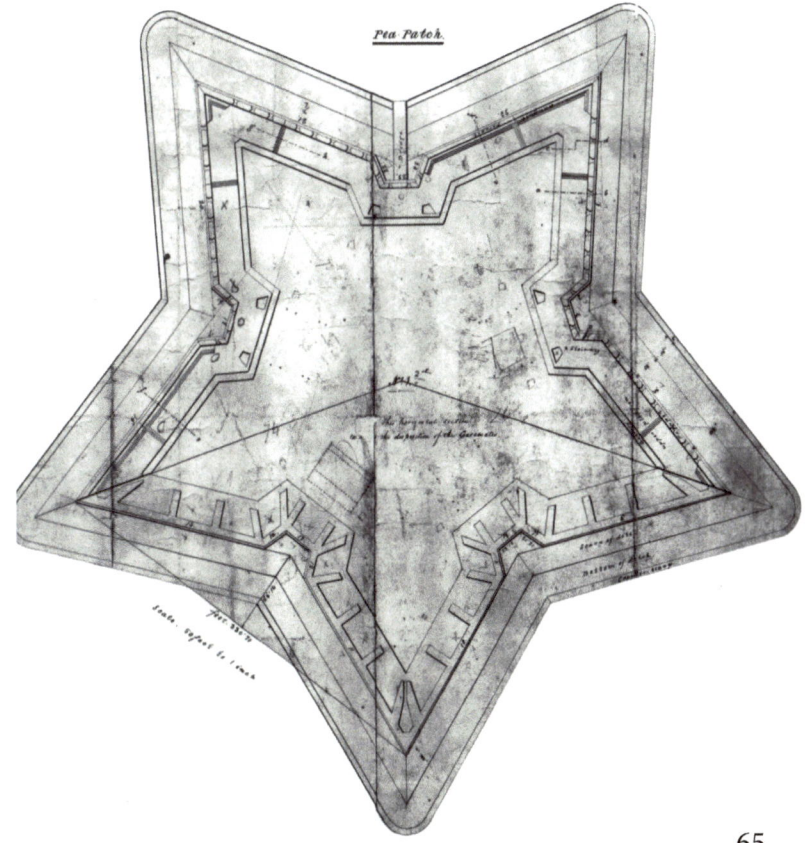

## Chesapeake Bay Orientations

Delaware's earliest settlements all rely on access to major trade markets via water routes. For southwestern Sussex County towns like Seaford and Laurel that means a focus westward, as the watersheds they sit on drain to the Chesapeake, not the Delaware, Bay. (cont. on pg. 94)

**Hearn & Rawlins Mill, Seaford**
**Original built c. 1760**

**Looking west from the "Wading Place"**
**ford crossing of Broad Creek, Laurel.**

Bishop Peter Spencer, whose Wilmington gravesite is marked by this statue, is considered the father of Delaware's independent black church movement. He founds the African Union Methodist Protestant Church in 1813. (cont. on pg. 95)

**Old Stone Tavern, Little Creek, built 1822**

It's never actually been a tavern, though locals refer to it as such. Records show it has always been a home. Elijah McDowell, the builder, must be a social fellow for this nickname to stick! He runs a store in Little Creek and deals in shipping grain, so he certainly knows all the farmers in the area. (cont. on pg. 95)

**19th century
chondrometer
(grain scale)**

*The Vesta* offers the first steamboat service between Wilmington and Philadelphia. Built by Joseph and Francis Grice of Kensington, PA, she is launched at Grice's Shipyard in Philadelphia on April 23, 1812. (cont. on pg. 96)

Chesapeake & Delaware canal opens 1829; Easternmost lock shown here. (cont. on pg. 96)

**Wilmington fêtes hero Marquis de Lafayette at Town Hall October 6, 1824.**

Marquis de Lafayette, the last surviving major general of the American Revolutionary War, starts his Grand Tour of the US in July 1824. By early October he makes his way to Delaware. Stops include a midday reception at Wilmington's Town Hall. Next, a visit to the Louviers estate of Victor Marie duPont, also in Wilmington (**lower left**, original stone gatehouse). Finally, a wedding at the home of Senator Nicholas van Dyke in New Castle. (cont. on pg. 96)

## Colonial Hearths

Notice there is a window on the left side within the fireplace in Wilmington's Hendrickson house. Why? What are the two cone-shaped objects attached to the back of the hearth at Odessa's Wilson-Warner house? How did the dutch oven, seen prominently in front of the hearth at New Castle's Old Dutch House, come into use? (cont. on pg. 97)

Hale-Byrnes House

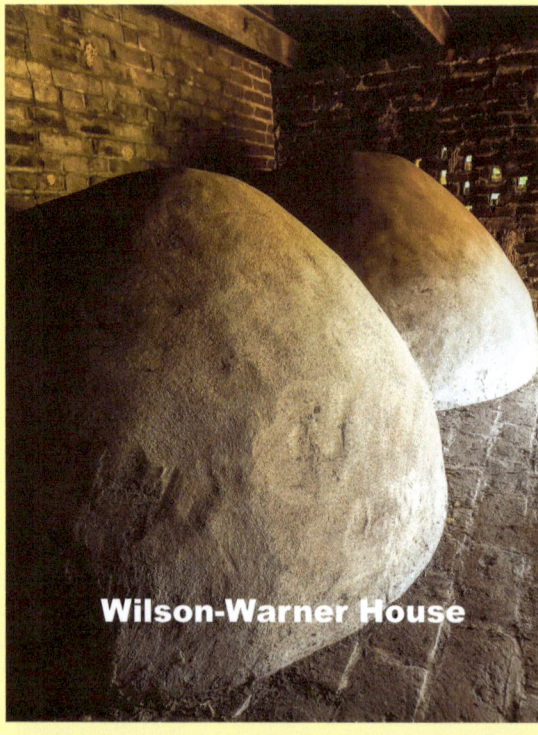

Wilson-Warner House

Old Dutch House

Hendrickson House

**Eight-Square Schoolhouse opens in 1836.**

Delaware becomes the second state in 1829 to establish a permanent system of free district public schools. This octagonal building is known locally in Cowgill's Corner as the Eight-Square Schoolhouse. (cont. pg. 97)

# Notes on Photographs

**Page 6 Cape Henlopen Storm** Where did the name "Delaware" come from? From Samuel Argall, the second European sea captain known to have visited Delaware Bay. Argall was employed by the Virginia Company, when on August 17, 1610, he was blown from his course on a voyage from Virginia to Bermuda, and took refuge from the weather behind Cape Henlopen.

The headland was then nameless, indeed non-existent, on his charts, and the bay behind it he named for his master, Thomas West, Baron De La Warr, the governor of Virginia. The headland lost this name, but the bay retained it, and from the bay the name traveled to the river that fed it, to the Indians on its banks and, later, to the state formed of the three lower counties on the western shore.

**Page 7 Lenape Fur Trading** Beaver skins were the main fur initially traded but were soon depleted on the peninsula. After 1640 the Lenape increased the amount of maize planted to sell to the Swedish colonists. The Swedes were concentrating their planting on tobacco for export, and bought maize from these Lenape foragers at lower costs than the value of tobacco. In this way the Lenape gained trade goods while not having to deal with the problem of food storage. (Collection Nanticoke Indian Museum)

**Page 7 Lenape Village Model** by John and Stanley Swientochowski, 1994, gift of Terry Wrightson, Collection of Delaware Historical Society

**Page 8 Kalmar Nyckel** What led to the founding of the New Sweden colony in North America? The commercial ambition of Swedish statesmen and their attempts to interest Dutch merchants in the copper trade. Copper mining was one of the most important industries in Sweden during the first half of the seventeenth century. The copper trade was a large source of income to the Swedish government, so it was always seeking new markets for the red metal.

In 1636 a coalition of Dutch businessmen, backed by capital (half from Holland, half from Sweden,) formed "The Swedish South Company" for copper trade as well as colonization on the South River (today's Delaware Bay). They would compete directly with the Dutch West India Company, which had already made inroads into that region.

Peter Minuit had been employed by the Dutch West India Company as General Director of their New Netherland colony from 1625-1632. He'd been recalled to Holland due a change in policy and dumped unceremoniously. He was aggrieved enough to be motivated to join The Swedish South Company, and was extremely knowledgeable about the South River terrain, inhabitants, customs, etc. The New Sweden coalition saw in Minuit the perfect candidate to lead its copper trade venture.

On December 31, 1637, Minuit's expedition set out from the Dutch island, Texel, aboard the *Kalmar Nyckel*, accompanied by the *Fogel Grip*. We know nothing about the journey across the Atlantic—Minuit's diary and log are lost but the ships reached the Delaware in good condition and sailed up the bay about the middle of March, 1638.

Minuit's instructions were to sail up to the Minquas Kill (today's Christina River in Wilmington), where he was to establish communications with the Indians. Having done so he was to explore the river as far as the Sankikan Kill (present day Trenton, NJ), and buy the land on the west side of the Delaware between the two streams. He was to erect the Swedish coat-of-arms at the northern and southern limits of the land, which was then to be called New Sweden. His base of operations was to be the Minquas Kill, where he was to erect a stronghold, giving it, with the firing of cannon, the name of New Stockholm. He was to begin the beaver trade with the Indians and buy cattle, horses, sheep, goats and pigs at New Amsterdam for the establishment of his colony.

Having made a beachhead according to these particulars, Minuit left the Delaware some time in June on board the *Kalmar Nyckel*. (Courtesy Kalmar Nyckel Foundation)

**Page 9 Aerial of Ft. Christina** In 1638, Swedish and Finnish colonists from the ships *Kalmar Nyckel* and *Fogel Grip* established a timber-and-earth fort along the Christina River on what is today's Seventh Street Peninsula in Wilmington. Named Fort Christina after the then 12-year-old queen of Sweden, it was the first Swedish settlement in America and the first permanent non-native settlement in Delaware.

Between 1638 and 1655, the profitable fur trade helped increase the settlement's population to 300. In 1655, however, the Dutch, looking to strengthen their control of the fur trade from the Delaware River to the Susquehanna Valley in Pennsylvania, attacked and quickly captured Fort Christina, renaming it Altenae. Despite the Dutch invasion, the population of the settlement remained predominantly Swedish. When Delaware fell to the English in 1664, the king's soldiers garrisoned the fort, but it was the Swedish settlement which remained the heart of the village that spread along the banks of the Christina and became, in the next century, Wilmington.

**Page 9 Interior of Swedish Log Cabin** Today, few people realize that the log cabin, the most "American" of building types, was introduced to the New World by European settlers. This one-room log dwelling was originally located on Old State Road Station in New Castle County. The structure was built in the late seventeenth or early eighteenth century. Mentioned in the 1720s will of Jasper Yeates, the house was likely standing prior to that date.

This type of house was introduced to America by Swedish and Finnish colonists who settled in 1639 at Fort Christina, now Wilmington. The round logs, v-notching, wide spaces between logs, clapboard gables and sharply peaked roof establish this as a Swedish-style structure. The house is constructed of white oak logs which are fitted without benefit of nails or tree nails (pegs).

Spaces between the logs are chinked with a mixture of mud, oat hulls, and grass. Resting on a stone foundation, the building originally had a crawl space between the floor and the earth. The shelf was used as sleeping quarters for children or as storage space. The brick chimney and fireplace were influenced by English design. (Collection of Delaware Agricultural Museum)

**Page 10 Hand-Hewn Beam** It seems unlikely that slave owners would grant slaves access to offsite sawmills of any sort. (Courtesy Milford Historical Society)

**Page 10 Causey Mansion Slave Quarters** One unique aspect of Milford, DE's Causey Mansion is a well-preserved slave quarters. Daniel Rogers owned the estate from 1797-1806. His probate inventory (d. 1806) listed large numbers of bricks, suggesting that this building was then under construction (he owned about fifteen slaves). The outbuilding served as shelter for the house servants and included one lower room with a brick floor and a large fireplace. One interesting feature of the slave quarters is a large scooped-out dent in the wall at the base of a ladder stairway. This modification was made, so legend has it, to permit one of the servants, who was not a small woman, to get up to her room. (Courtesy Causey Refresh)

**Page 11 Slave Mannequin** (Collection John Dickinson Mansion/State of Delaware Human and Cultural Affairs)

**Page 11 Interior of Barratt's Chapel, Frederica** Harry Hosier, an African American called "Black Harry," was a traveling companion of Francis Asbury. In 1781, says University of Delaware's James E.

Newton, Hosier preached a sermon at Barratt's Chapel on the barren fig tree: "The circumstance was new, and the white people looked on with attention." Hosier became well-known along the Eastern Seaboard, preaching for more than 30 years. (Courtesy Peninsula-Delaware Annual Conference Commission on Archives and History).

**Page 12 Ft. Casimir, New Castle / Dutch House interior** Johan Printz had been governor of New Sweden for 4 years already when Peter Stuyvesant was brought in as the new governor of New Netherlands (New York City) in 1647. Stuyvesant came into a tense situation that was only escalating. Printz had written to his superiors that the Dutch were destroying New Sweden's trading, arming the natives with guns to win their loyalty and then stirring up the natives against the Swedes, and buying up the very same parcels of land from the natives that the Swedes had previously purchased.

In reality the Swedes were also pursuing the very same means, but with less success. Stuyvesant came to the South River (Delaware Bay) in person in 1651 "to preserve and protect the company's rights and jurisdiction." He'd caught wind that Printz had secretly bought land titles from a sachem named Waspang Zewan. Stuyvesant approached Zewan directly to purchase the same land—both sides of the Delaware from Christiana Creek to Bombay Hook—without mentioning Printz's dealings.

Sure enough, Zewan was happy to oblige, and denied ever having sold any lands whatsoever to the Swedes. That event led Stuyvesant to conclude that another fort was needed to solidify Dutch presence in the area. He built Fort Casimir one Dutch mile from Fort Christina on the Delaware side of the river, and stationed a garrison with cannon and two ships there. But not without a fight. The Swedes overran the fort in 1654, and renamed it Fort Trefaldigheets—Trinity.

Stuyvesant personally circled back on September 11, 1655 to lead the Dutch troops who retook the fort, and kept it out of Swedish hands for good after that. That fort was the beginning of today's town of New Castle. (Courtesy New Castle Court House Museum)

**Page 13 Ryves Holt house, Lewes** Two boats of Englishmen were shipwrecked in 1657 near the Hoerenkill Creek (today's Lewes and Rehoboth Canal). They were captured by Lenni Lenape and freed when a ransom was paid by the Dutch. The following year, the Dutch decided to take action to protect their land on this portion of the South River (Delaware River) and, in particular, their town (previously called Swanendael, now Hoerenkill.)

Dutch colony governor Alexander d'Hinoyossa, William Beekman, and twenty soldiers were sent to purchase additional land from the Lenape. On June 7, 1659, the Lenape deeded to the Dutch all of the land between Cape Henlopen and Bombay Hook, extending inland/westward about thirty miles.

The Dutch erected a fort, but in 1664 Englishman Sir Robert Carr swept through to claim the land for the Duke of York, and destroyed or seized all the property of the "41 souls" living there at the time.

The house we today call the Ryves Holt House, shown on pg. 13 of this book, was built the following year, but not by him.

By 1673 the community the English had renamed Whorekill had developed into a port for shipping of grains, meat, and timber for ships. That year, magistrates of the first court tried to straighten out the land grants and define the plot of the town. Edmund Cantwell, first High Sheriff under the English, apparently planned the first streets. Maryland's Lord Baltimore saw the development unfolding, and sent soldiers to raid and burn the town. The Ryves Holt house is one of the few buildings that managed to survive that raid.

Between 1671 and 1681, thousands of acres were surveyed and granted mostly to men with English names. Shortly after Lord Baltimore's raid, the Dutch regained authority of the area for a short time before a treaty was established granting the land to the English.

After William Penn's arrival to New Castle in 1682, he renamed the lower three counties of Pennsylvania (now Delaware) New Castle, Kent, and Sussex and gave Lewes its name. Eventually, the Ryves Holt House was purchased in 1723 by its namesake, who served as the first Chief Justice of Delaware from 1745 until his death in 1763. This house is thought to be one of the oldest homes in Delaware. (Courtesy Lewes Historical Society)

**Page 13 Aerial Photo Bowers Beach** Bowers Beach, one of the earliest settlements along the Delaware Bay, was named "Whitwell's Delight" in the late 1600s by Francis Whitwell. At that time, the tract contained 834 acres of woodland and 540 acres of meadow. In 1685, William Frampton acquired the property and called it "Dover Peers". Frampton died, and the land was sold to William Bassett. Some years later, 420 acres of Whitwell's Delight was owned by Nathaniel and Mary Hunn. Nathaniel died, and in 1734 his children sold the 420 acres to John Bowers. Since August 16, 1734, the area "between the mouths of the St. Jones and Murderkill Rivers" has been known as Bowers Beach.

**Page 14 Kingston-Upon-Hull, Dover** Kingston-upon-Hull is an early example of a Delaware estate built along Kent County's St. Jones River. It is typical of the large, slave-worked plantations that supported a rural aristocracy along Delaware's rivers and bays, when the peninsula's interior was still wilderness. The tract that Kingston-upon-Hull occupies was patented in 1671, but the building's date of construction is unknown. The dwelling has sometimes been called Town Point, and nearby Dickinson Mansion has been called Kingston-upon-Hull.

In a 1677(78?) land survey done for owners John Briggs and Mary Philips, Walter Wharton clarifies Kingston-upon-Hull as "being the Land and plantation whereon they now Dwell *[sic]*," not the Dickinson Mansion, and furthermore describes the borders "dividing this from the Land belonging to the Towne point." Early 20th century historians mistook Kingston-upon-Hull for Kent County's first courthouse. The first court for St. Jones County (now Kent County) was in fact held in Edward Pack's house on Towne Point, next door. Kingston-upon-Hull was always a home, owned by the Dickinsons starting in 1733, and for many generations after.

**Page 15 Tobacco Plug and Pipe** The *Kalmar Nyckel* had shipped tobacco back to Sweden on its earliest return trips; New Sweden was expected eventually to become the main source of tobacco for the homeland. By the time of English colony governor Edmund Andros (in office 1673-1680), the chief produce of his Delaware River territory was provisions of all sorts, especially wheat, Indian corn, peas, beef, pork, fish, tobacco, furs (especially beaver,) timber, and various wood products such as planks and pipe staves, as well as horses, according to his testimony on a trip to England in 1678. Corn and wheat were staples, the crops most often grown for sale.

By the time of William Penn's arrival in the colonies in 1682, tobacco grown in Kent and Sussex counties remained, as it was before Penn's arrival, the most profitable local crop and chief export commodity to England. Debts and other obligations in Kent and Sussex counties were frequently stated in amounts of tobacco. By 1700, Kent surpassed the other counties in tobacco production. But growing tobacco for sale was abandoned by the time of the Revolution. Tobacco is an extractive crop; planted year after year in the same land it is hard on the soil. It is probable that after several generations of tobacco growing farmers were discouraged to find their yields decreasing. (Courtesy Old Library Museum/New Castle, DE)

**Page 15 Smokehouse** Every family kept its own cows and salted, cured and smoked its own bacon, beef, herring, shad, venison and mutton. The smokehouse, dairy and poultry house were appendages to all plantation homes. (Courtesy Buena Vista Conference Center, New Castle)

**Page 16 Immanuel Church, New Castle** Immanuel Church was founded in 1689 in New Castle, making it one of the oldest Episcopal parishes in the United States and the first parish of the Church of England in Delaware – which was still Pennsylvania at that point. Work on the church started in 1703 and was mostly complete by 1708. Massive work was done on the church in 1820 by noted architect William Strickland, who added the bell tower. (Courtesy New Castle Historical Society)

**Page 17 Kent County Courthouse, Dover** The St. Jones court, which met for the first time in June 1680 at Edward Pack's home in Town Point, served the newly formed Fourth Judicial Circuit of the Duke of York. Captain Anthony Brockholls, New York-based governor of the colony, split it off from the Third Judicial Circuit held in Whorekill (Lewes). The First Judicial Circuit was at New Castle, the Second, at Upplands (today Upland, PA).

When William Penn took over control of the Pennsylvania portion of the colony in 1682, he renamed St. Jones to Kent County, and Whorekill to Sussex. Fourth Judicial Circuit courts were held at Town Point till 1688, when the courthouse moved to the "Ordinary" of James Maxwell, on the first site of Dover Water Works, where court sessions were held until a courthouse was built in 1697 on the Green, on the site of the modern courthouse.

**Page 18-19 Old Swedes Church, Wilmington** It's one of the oldest churches in America. Old Swedes Church was actually built by English workmen and has few Swedish characteristics, though its construction was overseen by Swedish reverend Eric Bjorck. Mason Joseph Richardson of Philadelphia built the foundation of rubble stone, assisted by sons Joseph, William and John. The church wardens paid them 86 pounds silver, in addition to "sufficient Meat, Drink, Washing and Lodging [sic]."

Bjorck and the wardens contracted John Smart and John Britt of Philadelphia for carpentry, but Britt "failed" his partner, and Smart worked alone until John Harrson, also of Philadelphia, was hired to do all the inside carpentry. The committee brought in a glazier from Holland, and Matthias de Foss, "a smith of our own folk," prepared wrought iron letters painted red to be used in inscriptions on the north, south, east and west walls. The various crews completed the church by June 1699. (Courtesy Old Swedes Foundation)  (Hundreds map: Pomeroy and Beers Atlas of 1868/collection University of Delaware Library)

**Page 20 Collins-Sharp house, Odessa** Johan Risingh, the last governor of New Sweden, identified the river we know today as the Appoquinimink as 'Apoquenema Kill,' possibly from a Minquas tribe name for it. Both the Swedes and the Dutch were attracted to the area for its navigable location and had hopes of establishing a trading route with 'Mary-land' to the west. Alexander d'Hinoyossa, during his short term (1664-1665) as Vice-Director at New Amstel (New Castle), built a plantation on a tract of land given to him at Appoquinimink and intended to reside there and engage in trading.

The British had other ideas. In 1665 Sir Robert Carr overthrew Fort Casimir, seized d'Hinoyossa's estate, and granted it to Captain Edmund Cantwell, later the first sheriff of New Castle County under the government of William Penn. The British established a roadway, "Old Hermann's Cartroad," during the last years of the 17th century, connecting Bohemia Manor, MD with the village. The Collins-Sharp House, built in 1700, was actually moved to this spot in 1962 from its original location 16 miles away, along Road 493 on Thoroughfare Neck near Taylors Bridge. It's also been known as the Vogel House and the Collins-Johnson House. (Courtesy Historic Odessa Foundation, Inc.)

**Page 21 Kitts Hummock Scene** It was originally named "Kidds Hammock" after legendary pirate Capt. William Kidd. Rumor has it, Kitts Hummock (a hummock is a wooded knoll in a marsh or near a beach) was one of his Delaware Bay stops where he buried treasure.

Kidd's most famous haul resulted from a January 1698 takeover of the *Quedagh Merchant*, a 500-ton Armenian sailing the Indian Ocean, laden with gold, silks, and spices.

Kidd sailed the *Quedagh Merchant* for Anguilla in the West Indies, arriving in April 1699. He learned that he had been denounced as a pirate back in Britain. He left the *Quedagh Merchant* at the island of Hispaniola (where the ship was possibly scuttled; in any case, it disappeared) and sailed north in a newly purchased ship, the *Antonio*. He first appears on the record in Delaware in May 1699, anchored off the coast of Horekill (Lewes).

Colonial law forbade importation of goods from the East Indies—a law clearly aimed at pirates and privateers. Nonetheless, five Horekills residents boarded Kidd's ship and purchased a large quantity of goods from him.

The Earl of Bellomont, then colonial governor of New York, reported to London that Kidd had with him "a vast treasure, and had sent his boat on to the Horekills where he was supplied with what he wanted and from which the people went on board of him."

The five men who met Kidd eluded the Horekill tax collector and had already fenced their goods before the authorities caught wind. Penn managed to apprehend the group as accessories to pirates and promoters of illegal trade.

Kidd, meantime, continued up the Delaware coast. In addition to Kitts Hummock he was rumored to have left a buried stash at Woodland Beach.

**Page 21 Pilot Boats and Pirates** A favorite and most successful ruse of corsairs was to enter the Delaware capes under English colors and signal for a pilot, who, on approaching, was captured. The pilot boat was then manned and stationed within the capes; incoming vessels were met and easily captured by this innocent-looking guide. (collection of Lewes Maritime Museum)

**Page 22 Three Lower Counties** secede from the rest The "territories," as they were referred to, were to be governed by a separate Assembly consisting of representatives from the three counties but would still acknowledge the provincial governor of Pennsylvania's authority. This form of government continued right up till the State of Delaware adopted a separate constitution in 1776.

The events leading to a separate assembly revolved around constant power struggles between William Penn's council and the lower counties over respective powers and rights. Too often, officers were appointed for the lower counties without consulting the wishes of the county representatives. Delawareans saw Penn's claim to tax revenues from their soil and trade as a wedge between them and the Crown, and Penn's development of richer, more populous cities to the north, (and especially the fast-growing commercial center of Philadelphia) as a threat to their political and economic security.

The first separate assembly was held in November 1704 at New Castle. (Collection New Castle Historical Society)

**Page 23 The Green, Dover** The 1717 Delaware Assembly meeting at New Castle appointed three commissioners to lay out the town of Dover, to be completed by March 10, 1718. The commissioners accommodated William Penn's original 1683 plan by leaving the courthouse (which had been built some time before 1697 on the site of the modern Kent County courthouse) in place in the northwest corner of a courthouse square which extended to the south and east.

The backbone of the street grid was King's Highway (now State Street). Penn's plan proposed 200 acres allotted to the town siting; only about 125 were used. John Mifflin bought 69 of the remaining 75 acres and sold them to Nicholas Ridgely in 1748. This land is still owned by his descendants and is known as "The Ridgely Farm." John Lindsay bought the courthouse lot, including courthouse and jail, in 1722.

**Page 24 Plank House, Smyrna** Founded by 1705 where the King's Highway forded a navigable creek, Duck Creek Crossroads (today Smyrna) was the oldest settlement in northern Kent County. The village soon became a thriving community of merchants who shipped grain, lumber, peaches, staves and fertilizer to northern markets. Shipbuilding became a prominent business, and tanneries, fruit-drying plants and lime-kilns flourished. By the 1850s, Smyrna was the most important port between Wilmington and Lewes.

The plank house shown originally stood on what is now N. Main Street. In deteriorated condition by the 1950s, it was rescued and brought to The Lindens (the miller's house on Duck Creek, b. 1765) in 1962. In the 1990s, the Plank House was moved to the Smyrna Museum and restored. (Courtesy Smyrna Museum)

**Page 24 Short's Landing, Smyrna** Before the railroads arrived, overland travel was difficult at best. Delaware was dependent upon water routes for transportation. Most of the towns and settlements developed along navigable waterways. Those that were set back from the Delaware Bay, such as Smyrna, soon developed a series of landing spots along the river routes from the town to the bay. These landings usually consisted of a pier, a store, a hotel and a few dwellings. Short's Landing is the only one left besides Brick Store Landing in Blackbird Hundred, New Castle County.

**Page 25 Parson Thorne Mansion, Milford** The Anglican clergyman Parson Sydenham Thorne, for whom this Georgian home is named, is acknowledged as a co-founder of Milford. He was the first resident rector of Christ Church in Milford, and built the church still standing today. Statesman John M. Clayton, Secretary of State under President Zachary Taylor, spent his childhood years here. Dr. William Burton lived here for at least part of his term of office as Delaware governor.

The building is architecturally significant as an 18th century plantation house whose interior was not altered– it remains today as it was built, with original corner cupboards, chair rail and raised paneling. The builders didn't have access to marble but still wanted to project an image of wealth and taste, and so even though the lintels above the windows are made of wood, they've been painted to simulate marble. (Courtesy Milford Historical Society)

**Page 27 Vincent Loockerman House, Dover** It's called Loockerman Hall in a nod to Vincent Loockerman, the original owner of this elegant Georgian style colonial plantation house. And it sits today surrounded by high rise dormitories on the campus of Delaware State University. Delaware State College was originally established as the State College for Colored Students by an act of the Delaware General Assembly in 1891 in response to the 1890 Morrill Land-Grant Act, which provided financial assistance to the individual states for the creation of colleges for African-Americans.

When the college was placed on its present site, the area was still a working farm. Loockerman Hall was used as the college's first building. For the first 70 years of the college's existence, the building was used for academic and dormitory space.

The Loockerman family is one of the First Families of Delaware. Dutchman Covert Loockerman arrived at New Amsterdam in 1633 and soon became "the richest man in North America, being worth 52,000 Dutch guilders or about $208,099." His son Jacob moved to Maryland's Talbot County, where he sired (among other children) Nicholas, who in turn moved to Kent County. In 1723 Nicholas bought from Andrew Caldwell a tract of land known as part of "The Range, lying at the head of St. Jones River," for 100 pounds, according to the land deed. Presumably he and his wife, Susan Emerson Loockerman, built this house soon thereafter. It was the early home of their son Vincent, a Revolutionary patriot whose own house, built in 1742, is a landmark in Dover.

"Here Mr. Loockerman lived in the easy style of the old-time Southern gentleman, and here he died," says Scharf's *History of Delaware* (1888). "He built a dam and sawmill at the head of St. Jones Creek, northeast of the house." (Courtesy Delaware State University)

**Page 28-29 New Castle Courthouse Built** The New Castle Courthouse is a 2½ story, early Georgian-style brick building. The building is composed of three sections built between ca. 1730 and 1845. The oldest section of the building is the central, five-bay block which was built between 1730 and 1731. The four bay wide east wing section was built in two stages, 1765 and 1802.

William Kelsey decided to escape from the New Castle jail in 1729 by setting a fire. His escape plot didn't succeed, but he did manage to burn down the first courthouse on this site in New Castle. The central section of the building that stands today was in use by 1732, when the representatives of the Penn family and Lord Baltimore met to determine boundaries for the three lower counties, centering the twelve mile arc for the northern boundary of Delaware on the center of the cupola.

The New Castle Courthouse served as the seat of the colonial assembly of the Three Lower Counties from its construction in 1732 until June 15, 1776. In addition to its function as a place of assembly for colonial and state government, the New Castle Courthouse served as the judicial facility for the colony.

Important in the development of the city of New Castle, the presence of the building held a great deal of symbolic value for prospective settlers and merchants to the area, as an emblem of stability, order, and the rule of law. It also served the community as a gathering place for religious services, balls and dances, education, and public discourse on issues of the day. (Courtesy New Castle Historical Society)

**Page 30 Willingtown Becomes Wilmington** Two political factions had developed in Willingtown (Wilmington) by 1740. Thomas Willing had the backing of the old Swedish families, decades out of power but nonetheless viewed warily by William Penn, and William Shipley led a newly emerging Quaker coalition. Shipley had moved into town in 1735 from Ridley Township, PA (just southwest of Philadelphia) and was trusted by the Penn family in religious, business and political affairs. When Thomas Penn, one of William Penn's sons who succeeded his father as colony proprietor, sent a charter for the borough (requested by Shipley), he rebuffed Willing by changing the name of the town to Wilmington. This is said to be a tribute to his friend Spencer Compton, Earl of Wilmington. William Shipley, not Thomas Willing, was elected the first burgess under the new charter. (Courtesy Delaware Historical Society)

**Page 30 First Seagoing Ship Built in Wilmington** The Swedes and Dutch were involved in shipbuilding on the Christina River for many decades before the Quakers, led by William Shipley, seized commercial control. But their crafts—barges, canoes, sloops—were not aimed at foreign trade.

Shipley was chief burgess of Wilmington 1739-40 and an early landowner. He was a force in establishing early Quaker worship in Wilmington and was also a man of many business ventures, including a brewery. He and partners Griffith Minshall, David Ferris and Joshua Way changed the local shipbuilding emphasis in 1740 with the building of *The Wilmington*. According to the custom of the day the businessmen furnished hogsheads of rum daily to the workmen building the ships—free of charge. There was never a shortage of labor.

*The Wilmington* set sail on its maiden voyage the summer of the following year for Jamaica carrying Brandywine ground flour, barrel staves, beef and dairy products. These were traded for rum, sugar and molasses, and Spanish gold and silver coin. Rivalry with New Castle—shipping port and port of call a mere six miles down the river—was thus set in motion with the launch of this brig.

Nearly all the leading citizens of Wilmington from 1741 to 1775 owned or were interested in one or more sailing vessels, the majority of which were built locally.

**Page 31 First Presbyterian Church, Wilmington** Built by Scots-Irish in 1740 on the east side of what is now Market St below 10th, but in that period was an area isolated far beyond the limits of rustic Willingtown. Ministers were so scarce that religious services were held only once a month. The church served as a center for educated Irish refugees, some of whom became teachers. Delaware's first governor, Dr. John McKinly, is buried in the church's cemetery.

It didn't take long for several members to withdraw from the first church, and in 1744 that group built the 2nd Presbyterian Church, on 5th and Walnut Streets. The First Presbyterian was removed in 1919 from the original site, when the Wilmington Institute Library was built there, to Park Dr. at West Street.

**Page 31 Oliver Canby Flour Mill, Wilmington** Wilmington's flour mills were not the earliest in colonial America, but by the eve of the Revolution (when the flour trade in general experienced tremendous growth,) the town had become the leading flour milling town of the colonies. Any milling center needed water power, waterways to major markets, and capital to grow. Wilmington had the first two from the start, but it wasn't until William Shipley forged a strong business community from the town's Quakers in the late 1730's that the capital coalesced. Miller Oliver Canby, of nearby Bucks County, noticed the change and moved to Wilmington in 1742, bringing his sound knowledge of the business along with him. He built the first mill of consequence on the lower Brandywine, buying up valuable mill property over the next 12 years. Canby was an active and successful businessman, but died quite suddenly at the age of 38 after a brief illness, in 1754. (Courtesy Ashford Capital Management)

**Page 32-3 Hunting/Trapping/Fishing** Kentucky rifle (Collection Biggs Museum); Oyster shell bucket (Collection New Castle Historical Society); Traps hanging on wall (Courtesy Historic Odessa Foundation, Inc); Bucket of crabs (Photo by the author)

**Page 34 USN Sloop of War Wasp, Lewes** The *USN Wasp* shown here was constructed in 1806 at the Washington Navy Yard and commissioned in 1807 under command of Master Commandant John Smith. Her single action of the War of 1812 came in October of that year. On the 13th, she exited the mouth of the Delaware River and, two days later, encountered a heavy gale which carried away her jib boom and washed two crewmen overboard. The following evening, *Wasp* came upon a squadron of ships and, in spite of the fact that two of their number appeared to be large men-of-war, made for them straight away.

She finally caught the enemy convoy the following morning and discovered six merchantmen under the protection of *HMS Frolic*, a standard 18-gun brig sloop of the Cruiser class. At half past eleven on the morning of October 15, *Wasp* and *Frolic* closed for battle, commencing fire at a distance of 50 to 60 yards. In a short, but sharp, fight, both ships sustained heavy damage to masts and rigging, but *Wasp* prevailed over her adversary by boarding her.

Unfortunately for the gallant little ship, a British 74-gun ship of the line, *HMS Poictiers*, appeared on the scene, and *Wasp* became a British prize.

Tom Ruggiero built this model in 2012; gift of Tom Ruggiero, Ship Model Society of New Jersey; Collection of the Lewes Historical Society; 2021.63

**Page 35 Cape Henlopen Lighthouse** The British built a crude wooden lighthouse on Cape Henlopen in 1725. In 1764, Philadelphia merchants hired Major Henry Fisher, one of Lewes' leading pilots, to select a more permanent site, in a pine forest about 1,550 feet inland from the ocean, and a stone structure went up by 1767. That same year, Fisher determined proper locations of the first buoys set in the Delaware River and Bay. The lighthouse shown in the photo is a replica, sited in a traffic circle at Rehoboth Beach.

**Page 36 Old Christ Church in Laurel and Prince George's Church in Dagsboro** These are two of only eighteen church buildings in Delaware erected before 1800. Both are superb examples of eighteenth-century church architecture in the English tradition, conceived for masonry but executed in wood, in an area where stone wasn't easily available. Prince George's most striking feature is the barrel-vaulted ceiling, constructed of wide pine planks spanning the nave, forming a cross with the transepts.

Both churches served as Anglican (Church of England) 'chapels-of-ease' for Maryland-based parishes that aimed to serve parishioners in their outlying areas. Prince George's was founded in 1755 to serve the outlying areas of Worcester Parish, and Old Christ Church was built 1770-2 in Laurel to serve Stepney Parish.

Neither became a part of Delaware's religious network until 1791, when the Episcopal Church in Delaware codified its formal structure. The chapels are therefore of interest as an illustration of the long Delaware-Maryland boundary dispute's influence on church affairs. (Prince George's Chapel interior courtesy Friends of Prince George's Chapel)

**Page 37 Mason-Dixon Boundary Marker** The Mason-Dixon Line, named for Charles Mason and Jeremiah Dixon, the men who surveyed boundaries between Maryland and Pennsylvania, is known as the dividing line between the North and the South. But at the time of their land survey, Delaware was part of Pennsylvania, known as the "Three Lower Counties." The survey was commissioned to settle border disputes between the Penns of Pennsylvania and the Calverts of Maryland. By 1682, for example, Lord Baltimore had granted over 19,000 acres of land to settlers in what is today lower Sussex County, DE but was then claimed by Maryland.

The Mason-Dixon line runs along the southern border of Pennsylvania and turns south at Delaware. And so, Delaware is actually east of the colonial property line first established in 1765.

To mark the lines they drew, Mason and Dixon placed 87 stones (81 originals remain) on the ground at one-mile intervals. Every 5 miles they placed a crownstone, such as this one at Marydel. The stones had "P" engraved on the Pennsylvania/Delaware side of the border and "M" engraved on the Maryland side. Mason and Dixon also verified Delaware's southern boundary from the Atlantic Ocean to the "Middle Point" stone (along what is today known as the Transpeninsular Line). They proceeded nearly due north from this to the Pennsylvania border.

**Page 38-39 Colonial Medicine** PHARMACEUTICAL BOTTLES: 18th century physicians were drawn to quicksilver. Such a curious substance. It must have seemed like something otherworldly. It's a metal, yet flows at room temperature. It doesn't adhere to anything. Of course it would cure.

And so doctors used mercury for the treating of all sorts of problems, including worms, to stop vomiting, hysterical disorders, hypochondria, asthma, and syphilis. We now know mercury causes neurological disorders, in addition to neuromuscular changes, tremors, and harm to the kidneys and the thyroid. Literary wit Thomas Rowlandson, in "The English Dance of Death" (1815), caricatures the apothecary in his shop: *Of this grand shop behold the Master / Who deals in Bolus, Pill and Plaister / See how his Visage he disposes, / As his hands measure out the doses, / While his round paunch most truly tells, / He never takes the Drugs he sells.* (Collection of Thomas Marvel)

SYRINGES: were also used to irrigate wounds with wine or alcohol. Sore throats could be sprayed with hot water using a syringe. And in cases of swallowed poisons, the physician "washed out the stomach" using a "gum elastick" tube attached to the syringe. (Collection of Thomas Marvel)

CAPITAL SAW: Physicians commonly purchased their surgical and related supplies from the apothecary. The third quarter of the 18th century was a period of evolution in the design of most major surgical implements. The capital saw is a good example.

Early 18th century physicians used very ornate open frame saws generally adapted from the braced frame saw cabinet makers used. By 1740, these saws became generally lighter and smaller. By 1765, the design illustrated by this 1780 saw emerged, and went on to become almost universal. Surgeons used a 'spanner' (or wrench) to change or tighten the blade. (Collection of Thomas Marvel)

DENTAL TOOLS: Prior to the 18th century, teeth extractions were the main means to address tooth decay. In addition, market fairs sold tinctures, tooth powders and abrasive dentifrices.

While the wealthy could afford trained dentists (starting toward the later part of the 1700s), rural folks depended on the village blacksmith, hairdresser, silversmith, or barber to help alleviate toothaches and pull teeth. "Tooth drawers" sometimes used such painful practices as string pulling and hot coals to get teeth out.

More commonly, the tooth drawer used a pelican or forceps to extract teeth, by exerting lateral force on the tooth. John Aitkin perfected the English key (bent shaft type of iron tooth key with molded stem and turned bone handle) in 1771, which rendered the extraction of teeth easier and less liable to fracture the jaw, teeth, or gums.

French dentist Pierre Fauchard, in his 1728 book "The Surgeon Dentist," introduced the idea of dental fillings as a way to treat cavities and suggested using amalgams, such as lead, tin, or sometimes gold for fillings. (Collection of Delaware Academy of Medicine: dental saw 2006.41.99; metal tooth key 2006.41.96; tooth key ivory 2006.41.93; sand dollar 2006.41.102)

MORTAR/PESTLE: Mortars are made from a variety of materials, including bronze, marble, wood, brass, glass and stone. Colonial era apothecaries would have numerous mortars and pestles of various sizes and materials in their shops for different tasks: large mortars were used for bulk material, smaller mortars for grinding fine powders. (Collection of Delaware Academy of Medicine: mortar & pestle on left 1989.4.6 John J. Reinhard Collection; mortar and wood pestle 1997.07.07 Pierre LeRoy Collection)

LANCETS/FLEAM: All three tools shown are bloodletting devices. The two on the left are spring-loaded lancets; the one on the right is a fleam. The word phleam came from the Greek phlebotome: phlebos (Greek for blood vessel) and tome (to cut). The fleam is the older device and was less precise than the lancet. The Borwick veterinary folding fleam shown here (ca. 1790-1830) was likely also used on humans. Doctors in the country made home visits and checked on both the human and animal patients. The spring lancet, developed in the 18th century, made a vein incision with a rapid spring-activated stroke of the cutting blade. It was far preferred for use on humans because of this precision. The lancet shown top left in the photo is the oldest in the Delaware Academy's collection. The lancet below it is a Wiegand and Snowden spring lancet (ca. 1821-1855). Metalsmith John Wiegand (1800-1878) and carpenter Thomas Snowden (1798-?) formed a Philadelphia based partnership in 1821 to manufacture these and other surgical instruments. (Collection of Delaware Academy of Medicine: Borwick fleam 1989.04.03 John J. Reinhard Collection; 18th century spring lancet 2006.16.04; Weigand & Snowden spring lancet 2019.900.08)

**Page 40 First Printing Press, Wilmington** James Adams, first printer in Delaware (and only one for 25 years!), arrived in Wilmington in 1761 after working more than seven years with Franklin and Hall in Philadelphia. His efforts promoted English influences in education. One of his first publications was "The Child's New Spelling Book," which sold for a shilling. The next year Adams issued a reprint of a popular English book titled "A New Guide to the English Tongue." This work was illustrated and contained fables as well as word lists, and "the rules of English grammar."

Adams printed the first paper money—30,000 pounds—voted by the Assembly of the new state of Delaware in 1775. The bills bore on their reverse side the legend: "To counterfeit is death." The best known issue from Adams' Wilmington press was the celebrated Discovery, Settlement and present State of Kentucke, by John Filson, which Adams printed in 1784. At least three of Adams' sons---James, Samuel, and John---became printers. (printing press courtesy New Castle Historical Society; five shilling note courtesy Harvard University Baker Library/Harvard Business School W363119-1; Wilmington Almanack fascimile courtesy Library of Congress)

**Page 41 Newark Academy, Newark** One of the oldest universities in the U.S., the University of Delaware traces its roots to 1743 when a petition by the Presbytery of Lewes, expressing the need for an educated clergy, led the Rev. Dr. Francis Alison to open a school in New London, Pennsylvania. In 1765, Rev. Alison's elementary and secondary school relocated to Newark, DE, as the Newark Academy. The first Academy building, long since torn down, was of stone, erected in 1776 from funds raised in part from England. When in September 1777 it became clear that British General Howe would march through Newark, the Academy trustees sent the institution's funds to Wilmington for safekeeping. However, those funds, along with New Castle County records, fell into British hands. After Howe's march, the Academy building was used as a shoe factory for the Delaware militia troops. Classes resumed in 1780.

**Page 42-3 Corbit House, Odessa** In 1731, permission was granted to Edmund Cantwell's son, Richard, to erect a toll bridge over the Appoquinimink Creek at Appoquinimink Landing. It was called Cantwell's Bridge, and the town took the same name. In 1767, William Corbit opened the first industry in the town, a tannery, and it continued in operation until the 1850s. Tanyards in Odessa, Wilmington, and elsewhere were necessary to produce the leather needed in an agricultural society for uses as varied as men's breeches and shoes and horses' harnesses. (Courtesy Historic Odessa Foundation, Inc.)

**Page 44-5 The Blacksmith** How many households could the average blacksmith serve? A Kent County roster of 29 probate inventories and estate accounts for 1774 shows one blacksmith listed.

Many blacksmiths were so small scale that they were required to practice many trades to make ends meet. William Coleman, active between 1794 and 1808 in Drawbridge, worked as blacksmith, silversmith, farmer, harness maker, and builder of ship masts.

Where did the Delaware blacksmith get his raw, slab iron? The Iron Hill area in western Pencader Hundred (New Castle County) was an area already known by 1673 to contain iron deposits; a map from that year labels the spot "Yron hill." One John Ball purchased a plot near St. James Church in Mill Creek Hundred in 1706, and built a bloomary furnace (an early smelting furnace) shortly afterward. Ball was a blacksmith by trade, as was often the case with early furnace operators. After the War of 1812, Sussex County's bog-iron industry started to reach the point where its products were sold through much of the middle Atlantic region. (blacksmith sign courtesy Milford Museum; background photo to it courtesy Delaware Agricultural Museum; boot scraper and lock both courtesy State of Delaware/Division of Historic and Cultural Affairs; farm implements courtesy Milford Museum; bread warmer courtesy Historic Odessa Foundation, Inc.)

**Page 46 John Dickinson Letters From a Farmer in Pennsylvania, Dover** John Dickinson was eminently placed to comment on the political world he was helping to construct. Trained as a lawyer, his scholarly writing style lent gravity to the cause for colonial liberty he championed.

Delawareans avidly read his tempered, reasoned denunciation of the Townshend Duties (a taxation without representation issue) in his 1767 "Letters From a Farmer in Pennsylvania," published in Philadelphia's Pennsylvania Chronicle. His "Letters" were reprinted in papers throughout the colonies and made Dickinson famous for his legal defense of American liberties. Benjamin Franklin added a preface to the republished London edition. The "Farmer's Letters" went on to be published in Paris.

This series was neither his first nor his last commentary on Great Britain's attempted infringement of its American colonies' liberties. The year before, he'd penned a masterly defense of the colonies in his "Address to the Committee of Correspondence in Barbados," which had censured the northern colonies for their opposition to the Stamp Act.

Dickinson was a deputy to the First Colonial Congress in 1765, and drew up its resolutions. By 1774, the clear, forceful logic of his writing voice reached full maturity. While serving that year as a member of the First Continental Congress, he produced in rapid succession "Essay on the Constitutional Power of Great Britain over the Colonies in America," "Address to the Inhabitants of Quebec," "The Declaration to the Armies," two petitions to the King, and "Address to the States."

From our modern perspective it might seem odd, then, that Dickinson opposed and refused to sign the Declaration of Independence. But he felt it was premature; he believed in constitutional procedure rather than revolution. This unpopular position cast a shadow over Dickinson's public service for several years. But in 1779 he returned to Congress from Delaware. Dickinson became President successively of the states of Delaware (1781-3) and Pennsylvania (1783–85). He owned homes in both.

In 1788 he published the 'Fabius' letters, advocating adoption of the new constitution, and in 1797 another round of 'Fabius' letters, the last of his political essays. Capping his long and distinguished career, John Dickinson - the "Penman of the Revolution" - published two volumes of his "Political Writings" in 1801.

In 1792 he was one of the delegates to the convention that framed the US Constitution. (courtesy State of Delaware/Division of Historic and Cultural Affairs)

**Page 47 George Read House, New Castle** Carefully coordinated mass meetings were held in each county. At these meetings speakers condemned British acts, called for a collection to aid the people in Boston who were impoverished by the closing of their port, recommended the establishment of county committees of correspondence, and urged the speaker of the assembly, Caesar Rodney, to convene the members quickly so they could choose delegates to Congress.

George Read, Thomas McKean, and Caesar Rodney were the final delegates. What did the First Continental Congress achieve? Two things: 1) it adopted petitions to England protesting the legislation passed by Parliament in retaliation for the Boston Tea Party, and 2) an agreement to boycott English goods. (courtesy Delaware Historical Society)

**Page 47 Thomas McKean Law Office, New Castle** Although Thomas McKean had made Philadelphia his permanent residence in May of 1774, he retained a New Castle residence and his membership in the assembly there. Delaware elected him to the first Continental Congress that fall, and he was annually re-elected until February 1783, the longest period of service of any member of that body. McKean was a member of the committee to state the rights of the colonies, a secret committee to contract for arms and ammunition importation, and a committee on the confederation of the colonies. As someone who practiced law in both Delaware and Pennsylvania, McKean offered up a personal role model for intercolonial cooperation.

**Page 48 Caesar Rodney Rides to Philadelphia** This bronze bas relief, centrally placed at a public square in Wilmington named for him, commemorates Caesar Rodney's ride to Philadelphia to cast the deciding vote for independence. It shows Rodney bursting onto the scene at Independence Hall.

Caesar Rodney is one of only two Delawareans to have a marble statue in the Rotunda of the Nation's Capitol. Even without that famous ride, Rodney was among the foremost of all Delawareans in the struggle for independence. But none of his tremendous achievements had the drama, the excitement, the heroic stamina reflected in that ride from near Dover to Independence Hall in Philadelphia. What happened on July 1 and 2, 1776, that has virtually canonized him as the greatest of Delawareans during the Revolutionary era?

In mid-June 1776, Rodney, who was Brigadier General of Kent County militia as well as a member of Congress, came home from the Congress in Philadelphia to help deal with a threatened Tory uprising. But by month's end, when time came for the final vote on Independence back in Philadelphia, Delaware's vote hung in the balance. Rodney's vote was needed to break the tie between Thomas McKean "for" and George Read "opposed." McKean dispatched a messenger to notify Rodney to return to Philadelphia. Rodney was at his Byfield estate near Dover. He promptly dropped everything, saddled up and rode the 86 miles back to Philadelphia, through a fierce thunderstorm, overnight without sleep and without stopping, save for changing horses. This noble act of self sacrifice, of putting service to his country above all else, has captured the popular imagination ever since.

**Page 49 Capital Moves to Dover** The Old State House is the second-oldest state building in the country (Maryland has the oldest). The second Kent County Courthouse was originally built on the site in 1722, after the 1697 Courthouse site was sold and the King George Inn took its place.

This second Court House of 1722 served during the Revolutionary period and became the State House as well in 1777, when Dover, an inland town, was made State Capital due to fears that New Castle might fall to British naval attacks too easily. The Georgian style Old State House we see today was built in 1787, using the existing bricks for a new foundation, "as there was not sufficient money for a stone foundation."

**Page 50 Delaware Regiment Musters** The Delaware Regiment first saw action at the Battle of Long Island, fighting with distinction, and then covered the Continental Army's withdrawal across New Jersey. In January 1777, after enlistments expired and Haslet died, the regiment reorganized under the leadership of Colonel David Hall, with many veterans rejoining.

For the next two years, the Delawares were part of the Main Army, fighting in the battles of the Philadelphia Campaign and at Monmouth. The regiment also joined in the assault at Staten Island, and selected men participated in the night attack at Stony Point. After eight years of service, the regiment returned to Delaware in January of 1783 and was mustered out later that year.

Forced to endure great hardship, the Regiment was widely acclaimed for its discipline and bravery. Virginia's Colonel Henry Lee wrote admiringly, "The State of Delaware furnished one regiment only; and certainly no regiment in the army surpassed it in soldiership."

**Page 50 Cooch's Bridge Battle** In September 1777, the British army under Sir William Howe marched through the northwestern corner of Delaware en route to Philadelphia. Not only for the few weeks when British troops were in Delaware, but also for the eight months that they occupied Philadelphia and controlled the Delaware River, the Delaware counties were on the front line of the war.

Knowing that a British army was moving by sea from New York to the Chesapeake, Washington marched his troops to Wilmington and then advanced to Red Clay Creek, expecting to face the British there as they came from their landing place on the Elk River. On September 3, 1777, Howe's army was advancing from Glasgow (then Aikentown) toward Christiana when it ran into a force of just under one thousand American light infantry in the woods along the road at the foot of lron Hill.

In this Battle of Cooch's Bridge, the role of the outnumbered Americans, commanded by William Maxwell, was to harass the main body of the British and make their advance difficult. At the end of the engagement, however, the British camped in the area for three days, bringing up supplies from their landing place and then struck off north to Kennett Square, in Pennsylvania, instead of northeastward to Wilmington.

**Page 51 Hale Byrnes House** George Washington bivouacked his 10,000 man army on the grounds around the Tatnall (today Hale-Byrnes) House in Stanton starting August 28, 1777. He expected British General Howe to march from the Head of Elk to Philadelphia in this direction, but after the September 3 skirmish at Cooch's Bridge, Howe veered west through Newark instead. On September 8, Washington moved his men toward Brandywine Springs.

Stanton is one of the oldest settlements in Mill Creek Hundred. Grist and sawmills used the water power of Red Clay and White Clay creeks as early as 1679. The place was called Cuckoldstown up to about 1768; local property owner Stephen Stanton lent his name to the spot after that. Washington used the Hale-Byrnes House, a 1750 Dutch-Colonial style building, as his headquarters during his time camped there. (Courtesy Delaware Society for the Preservation of Antiquities)

**Page 51 British Occupy Wilmington** On September 11, 1777, Washington was determined to prevent the British from capturing the American seat of government, Philadelphia. Taking up eastern positions along Brandywine Creek just north of the Delaware border, Washington mistakenly believed that his army blocked all fords across the Brandywine.

Hidden by heavy fog, Howe and an army of 15,500 British Regulars and Hessian troops moved into position. General Wilhelm von Knyphausen was ordered to 'amuse' the Americans' front at Chadds Ford as a distraction, while the bulk of Howe's forces crossed the Brandywine further upstream.

Washington's poor reconnaissance prior to the battle and his inability to understand the intelligence reports the day of the battle doomed his army. Howe was successful in capturing and occupying Philadelphia. Washington's army retreated to Chester, Pennsylvania.

The capture of Philadelphia would prove to be a hollow victory. The hoped for uprising by Pennsylvania loyalists never occurred. Also, Continental patrols limited supplies into the city to a trickle. Ultimately, the British were forced to abandon the city in the spring of 1778. Likewise, the British evacuated Wilmington after nine months, leaving in June of 1778 to focus on the southern theater of war. (Painting: 'British infantrymen of a royal regiment in an encampment,' ca. 1760; collection National Army Museum/London; Image 94819; NAM. 2001-12-35-1)

**Page 52 Barratt's Chapel, Frederica** Barratt's Chapel was one of at least 6 Methodist churches built in 1780. But unlike the others, Barratt's is considered the 'cradle of Methodism.' Local landowner Philip Barratt sold the parcel to a Methodist board of trustees in August 1780. He had met Freeborn Garrettson, a Methodist missionary, in 1778 when Garrettson was preaching in private homes in the area. Barratt and his friend, Waitman Sipple, were moved to form a Methodist Society, and in March 1780 started building a brick chapel on Barratt's land.

Francis Asbury and Thomas Coke were elected first Superintendents of the Methodist church in America on December 24, 1784 in Baltimore. They had first met each other only a month before, at Barratt's Chapel. For its first 60 years, the church's interior was roughly finished. There is some confusion as to whether the original floor was dirt or brick. Allen Clark, historian and author of "New Light on Old Barratt's," says it was either dirt or brick, but came to the conclusion it was probably brick. Barratt's deed of trust allowed African American members to hold meetings on designated midweek evenings, using only the upper gallery. It stipulated, furthermore, that three of the nine trustees must be present and that the worshippers "must not become boisterous." Two former Delaware governors—George Truitt and John W. Hall—are buried in the graveyard adjacent to the church. (Courtesy Commission on Archives and History of the Peninsula-Delaware Annual Conference of the United Methodist Church)

**Page 52 Old Bethel Methodist, Lewes** Rhodes Shankland spearheaded the formation of the Methodist Episcopal Church in Lewes and Rehoboth Hundred. The church incorporated locally in March 1788 and two months later, Shankland deeded "70 perches of land" to the church trustees. They built a frame church, Ebenezer M.E. Church, on South St. "where the Canary Creek crosses the street." Bethel M.E. Church was built about 1790 at 3rd and Market Streets. Francis Asbury noted in his journal on Oct. 23, 1790, "We have a chapel at Lewistown." This probably referred to Bethel, though he may have meant Ebenezer. The Lewes congregation met alternately at the two churches until Ebenezer was abandoned, and the entire site given over to be used as a graveyard.

**Page 53 Homespun Domestic Clothing** Spinning wheel (Collection of Milford Museum); Loom (Collection of John Dickinson Mansion/Delaware Dept of Human and Cultural Affairs); Flax heckle (Collection of Old Swedes Foundation)

**Page 54 Choptank Mill/Mud Mill, Marydel** The Choptank Mill in Marydel is an excellent example of that minority of mills in Delaware oriented westward for shipping their goods by their location on the Chesapeake Bay watershed. In addition to the Choptank River, where this mill sits at the confluence of Mud Mill Pond, the Nanticoke and the Pocomoke in southwestern Delaware are the state's other major rivers in that same watershed. The Choptank Mill is one of the best documented mills in Delaware, thanks to the efforts of historian Richard Alan Sehorn.

Millwright David Marsdin started up in 1756 on 10 acres of land, and mill operations continued at this same spot under various owners and mill structures until the Medford family sold it to the state in 1982. The building that occupies the site currently was built in 1926. The Medfords are noteworthy because, rather than simply letting the millworks rot after they shut down, they graciously donated the mill workings to the

Delaware Agricultural Museum and Village so that future generations will be able to appreciate what went into a gristmill concern.

**Page 55 First Gristmill in Delaware** Brandywine Creek got its name from Ashmond Stidham, who built the first mill in Wilmington in 1640. Stidham ground barley, and as a side venture produced "aquavit," an alcoholic beverage enjoyed by the inhabitants of Nordic countries since the early 1500s. Distilled from grain or potatoes and flavored with dill herb - or caraway seed - distillate, this yellow-hued, 80 proof (40% alcohol) drink is still produced today. The Stidhams made the first aquavit in Delaware using barley and water from the creek. So. How did Brandywine Creek get its name? Stidham's product is known by different names in Denmark and Sweden… it is called "Snaps", "Dram", or …"Brændevin."

**Page 55 Abbott's Mill, Milford** It didn't become Abbott's Mill until 1919, when Ainsworth Abbott and Joseph J. Smith bought it. On early maps of Cedar Creek Hundred, it's simply labeled 'grist mill.'

Nathan Willey, a local carpenter, bought seven acres of land from Levon Poynter in the fall of 1795 on what was then known as Bowman's Branch, two miles southwest of Milford. Seven years later, in April 1802, Willey and several of his neighbors presented a petition to the Court of General Sessions stating that he had "at a large expense erected, and just finished" a saw mill on the site. The petition requested that a new road be extended to the recently completed mill, citing the many advantages to the citizens of the neighborhood.

After 1808 Willey converted his mill to a gristmill, with a breast-shot waterwheel that drove two sets of 48" millstones, one for corn and the other for wheat, oats or buckwheat.

When Nathan Willey died in 1812, the mill was sold to James Owens and then to Isaac Riggs. The name Johnson's Mill stuck when James Johnson bought the mill in 1821, and both his son and grandsons continued the business after he passed. (Courtesy Delaware Nature Society)

**Page 56 The Golden Fleece Inn, Dover** Delegates to the ratifying convention gathered at The Golden Fleece Tavern, the same place where the state assembly sometimes met. Also known as Battell's Tavern and the place for community and government activities, this site became the center for important decisions during the American Revolution and the early years of independence. With no state capital building until 1791, the tavern became the place for the upper assembly's Legislative Council to meet. On December 7, 1787, 30 delegates, ten from each county, met to unanimously ratify the Federal Constitution, making Delaware "The First State".

**Page 57 Abolition Societies in Dover and Wilmington** In 1788-89 Abolition Societies arose in both Dover and Wilmington. Local Quakers in Camden, such as the Hunn, Jenkins, and Cowgill families, were well known for their efforts in support of abolition. Some served as conductors on the Underground Railroad, providing "safe houses" and passing fugitive slaves northward. Of particular note was John Hunn, the Chief Engineer of the Underground Railroad in Delaware. Hunn was responsible for the operation of the network that transported thousands of escapees through Delaware to Wilmington, and thence to freedom. He's buried in the cemetery adjacent to the Camden Friends Meeting House.

**Page 58 Old Sussex County Courthouse, Georgetown** As early as 1786 there had been popular pressure from Sussex Countians in the southwestern corner for a change of the Sussex County seat. The leaders of the movement claimed that Lewes, being at the extreme eastern side of the county and a full day's journey away for them, was not a convenient place for a majority of Sussex people. As a result of the continued uproar, in 1791 the State Assembly passed an act to purchase 100 acres of land—James Pettyjohn's old field—in the center of Sussex County and to erect on the new town grid a courthouse and a jail with pillory and whipping post.

In 1792, the newly established town was named Georgetown, in honor of George Mitchell, one of the commissioners appointed to carry out the Assembly's act. In 1793, the original courthouse was built at the expense of several private citizens, who were reimbursed from the proceeds of a 1795 lottery authorized by the State. This first courthouse was a small, cypress-shingled frame building very much like the two-story-and-attic dwelling house of the time. It followed two earlier buildings in Lewes, the last of which stood on St. Peter's Episcopal Churchyard. Both county offices and the courtroom were on the first floor. (Courtesy Georgetown Historical Society)

**Page 59 1792 Convention, Dover** The public voted in delegates, including long-time political stalwarts John Dickinson, Nicholas Ridgley, John Clayton, and Richard Bassett. The convention delegates assembled in Dover late in November and deliberated on the new constitution's fine points for a month. They drew up a draft, ordered it printed, submitted it to the General Assembly, and adjourned. In late May 1792 the convention members re-assembled, ostensibly to discuss any changes to the document they had offered to the Assembly at the end of 1791. Ironically, the new constitution was never put to the people for ratification but was simply adopted by the State. The convention adjourned June 12.

Major changes included the establishment of a separate Chancery Court and the expansion of the state tax base to include all taxpayers. John Dickinson, as convention president a bellwether of the group's direction, remained neutral in an attempt to include a prohibition of slavery in the document, believing the General Assembly was the proper place to decide that issue. Delaware's President was renamed Governor by the new constitution, which set the commencement date of the term to the third Tuesday in the January following an election, and limited governors to serving only three out of any six years.

Under the Delaware Constitution of 1776, the General Assembly consisted of The Legislative Council and the House of Assembly. 'House of Assembly' was a common name for lower houses of colonial legislatures and states under the Confederation. The name was changed by Delaware's 1792 Constitution, reflecting the new federal House of Representatives. The Legislative Council became the Senate. (Courtesy State of Delaware / Human and Cultural Affairs)

**Page 59 Bank of Delaware Founded** The charter limited its operations to fifteen years. Its formal name was "The President, Directors and Company of the Bank of Delaware." Joseph Tatnall, age 55, who had made his initial fortune running one of the early flour mills in Brandywine Village, was the bank's first president. The bank opened for business in August 1795 at the northwest corner of Fourth and Market Streets, a property owned by stockholder James Lea. The bank was in the black from the start; its first semi-annual dividend was 5 dollars a share.

The earliest section of the building shown here, the bank's second location, was originally constructed in 1815-16, with c. 1888 and 1907 alterations. The building was carefully taken apart, moved from its original 6th and Market Streets location in Wilmington and re-erected at Lovering Avenue in 1931-32. It had originally been designed to serve as both a banking house and a cashier's residence. (Courtesy Gordon, Fournaris & Mammarella)

**Page 60 Old Town Hall Bell, Wilmington** This bronze bell originally hung in the cupola of Old Town Hall, Wilmington from 1800 to 1875. The bell, cast in England, was purchased by Joseph Tatnall (1740-1813), a prosperous local miller and merchant who also purchased the clock for the building. As one of the tallest buildings in Wilmington for almost a century, the Town Hall and its tower became an important community focal point. The bell worked with the clock to strike on the hour but could also be rung manually as a fire alarm, to summon the citizenry to meetings, or to mark a period of public celebration or mourning. (Collection Delaware Historical Society)

**Page 61 Old Town Hall, Wilmington** The building's style reflects the preference for efficient, unobtrusive government and the Quaker ideal of unornamented design preferred by the Society of Friends, who had a large presence in the city at that time. For its first one hundred years, Town Hall served as the center for important governmental proceedings and community activities.

Town meetings, elections, exhibits, the naturalization of new citizens, court activities, and private gatherings all took place here. Numerous groups used Town Hall as their headquarters, including the Philosophical

Society, the Freemasons, the Library Company, and two early fire companies.

**Page 61 Yellow Fever Epidemic, Wilmington** W. C. Smyth began publishing the *Wilmington Mercury* newspaper in September 1798 in response to the yellow fever epidemic sweeping Philadelphia, New York City, and Wilmington. He printed the paper on a daily basis and delivered it free of charge. Each issue included a call for donations to the Board of Health to assist hospitals in caring for the sick. Items and cash donations could be dropped off at the Health Office located near Wilmington's town hall on Market Street. The *Mercury* then published the names of individuals and the items they donated to the Board of Health. Donations were also collected from outside of Delaware, for example, from Kent County, Maryland, and from Birmingham and Concord Townships in Pennsylvania.

The *Mercury* included in every issue the names of those who died in the previous 24 hours, in addition to counting the total number of deaths from August 7, 1798, when the disease first arrived in Wilmington. As of November 2, 1798, 229 adults and 23 children had died from the illness. Among the prominent citizens who died were James Lea, Sr., Major John Patton, Joseph Miller, Eleazer Macomb and his wife.

The *Mercury* also offered its readers advice for dealing with the epidemic, such as closing up homes and leaving the city until the epidemic eased, and airing out and whitewashing homes in order to fumigate them.

The *Wilmington Mercury* ceased publication sometime in November 1798 when the yellow fever epidemic abated as temperatures cooled. (Wilmington Mercury Collection Delaware Historical Society)

**Page 62 Colonial Clockmaking** *Beard clock:* Duncan Beard (1740-1797) was both a clockmaker and silversmith. The Scotsman bought a small one-acre piece of property two miles south of Cantwell's Bridge (modern day Odessa) in Appoquinimink, where he ran his business for 30 years. Beard was a charter member of the Masonic Union Lodge No. 5, chartered in 1765, the first Masonic organization in Delaware. The lodge initially met at Old Drawyers Church, where Beard was a prominent member. The present church was designed by Beard and built in 1773. The minutes of a 1766 Lodge meeting at the newly built Middletown hall show Beard was commissioned to make all the lodge's jewels, a tall clock, some candlesticks, and a chest (which were all destroyed in a 1918 fire, except the Secretary's jewels, which he had worn home by mistake.) In 1776 Beard made gun locks for the convention that met in New Castle to adopt a constitution for the new State of Delaware. (Tall Case Clock, circa 1780, mahogany, brass, steel, glass, iron, gold, bronze, 1958.057, Delaware Division of Historical and Cultural Affairs)

*Weaver clock:* This tall case clock was made between 1795-1810, with 8-day, key wound movement. The case is attributed to John Janvier, Jr. and the brass works are by Christopher Weaver (working 1780s–1815); Weaver also built clockworks for John Janvier, Sr. A series of horizontal boards, rather than a single vertical board, distinguish the backs of his cases. Janvier's method was copied by other case makers in the area. Highly scalloped doors, no two alike, mark Odessa-area clocks. Duncan Beard also worked with Janvier, Sr. Housed in a 9-foot-tall mahogany case attributed to Janvier Sr, a Beard clock remains in the Odessa house of William Corbit (1746–1818), for whom it was made. (Courtesy Delaware Historical Society)

After his partnership with Beard dissolved, Weaver ran a business in Georgetown for a time. But he moved back north—the clock shown here is signed "Chris. Weaver / New Castle." He was a neighbor of Duncan Beard's when he served as one of two witnesses and executors of Beard's will when the latter died in 1797 in Appoquinimink.

Weaver/Beard clock: This clock is a fine example of the decorative details and construction techniques of the Janviers' Rococo style in Delaware. These include scalloped carving within the waist door and base panel. (Collection Biggs Museum)

*Crow clock:* Thomas Crow of Wilmington made this tall flat-top case clock about 1800. The case is mahogany and tulip poplar. His father George was one of Wilmington's early clockmakers. The father appears in the record in 1746 when he was elected high constable of the borough of Wilmington. He continued his business till 1770. Thomas, the oldest son, was Wilmington's town clerk in 1771, one of the assistant burgesses in 1778-80, and borough assessor in 1784-5. He worked in Wilmington til 1808, when he moved to West Chester, PA. About 1810 he returned to Wilmington, bought a property on the south side of 2nd St, just east of Market, and worked there till his death in 1824. Thomas Crow trained the last generation of Wilmington clockmakers, among them John Crow and Jonas Alrichs. (Delaware Division of Historical and Cultural Affairs)

**Page 63 DeBraak Sinking, Lewes** The British Consul in Philadelphia was informed of the disaster and sent two salvage brigs to raise the sunken ship. This contributed to rumors of gold treasure aboard: the boat was old, had been poorly retrofitted, and would never be seaworthy again, at least not for the purposes of the British Navy. So why were they going to all this trouble? Gossips whispered that it may have been in response to stories about the surviving sailors, said to have paid for rooms in local hotels with gold doubloons. Rumors. Gossip. Stories. "There were never any official statements about treasure made by the survivors in Admiralty court or during the prize proceedings," points out Donald Shomette in 'The Hunt for HMS De Braak,' "nor by the British consul in Philadelphia, Admiral Vandeput, the Royal Navy , or any representatives of the Britsih government."

The British eventually wrote the *De Braak* off as a total loss. But despite the facts, a legend had been created, capturing the imagination of treasure seekers for years to come.

Over thirty attempts to find and raise the *De Braak* failed, until the 1980's. Located with sonar, she was then finally lifted out of the water with a crane. This was accomplished only after two competing companies fought in court to work the wreck. The company that won the right to excavate the ship went about this work in a very haphazard way. Some observers reported that the salvage team simply threw overboard anything that did not look like treasure, including, for example, a Brodie galley stove, standard on British military ships only from 1767-ca.1810. The firm was also criticized for their improper disposal of the human remains. (courtesy Delaware Division of Historical and Cultural Affairs)

**Page 63 Dupont Gunpowder Works Founded** What drove Eleuthere Irenee du Pont de Nemours to site his gunpowder mill along the Brandywine Creek in Wilmington? His father, a well connected French diplomat, had urged Irenee to locate his powder works near the new capitol, Federal City. Proximity to that would be an advantage in securing government business. The younger du Pont was not convinced, though, and explored the Hudson River area of New York, New Jersey, and Philadelphia. He returned to the Federal City area, and scoured nearby possibilities in Maryland and Virginia. "The country, the people, the location are all worthless," he wrote his father in disgust in September 1801. "I shall stop off in Wilmington for a day to see the Brandywine."

A small colony of Frenchmen lived in the Wilmington area, one of whom, Peter Bauduy, had promised to help fund du Pont's powder plant if the latter would locate near Wilmington. That probably tipped the scales. The 95 acre farm du Pont chose to purchase was well stocked with willow trees, the best variety for charcoal, had a great deal of land already cleared, and had a fast, steady flow of water from the creek at that point. (Courtesy Hagley Museum & Library)

**Page 64 Commodore Thomas MacDonough Childhood Home, Middletown** One point to be made about the title "Commodore": MacDonough began to be called this after the battle on Lake Champlain, but it wasn't an official rank used by the Navy then. He was Captain MacDonough. "Commodore" is more of an honorary, affectionate title.

Thomas MacDonough was the son of Dr. Thomas and Mary McDonough. A veteran of the American Revolution, the senior McDonough served with the rank of major at the Battle of Long Island and was later wounded at White Plains. Raised in a strict Episcopal family, the younger Thomas was educated locally, and by 1799, was working as a store clerk in Middletown (Delaware, not to be confused with Middletown, CT, where he is buried).

At this time, his elder brother James, a midshipman in the US Navy, returned home having lost a leg during the quasi-war with France. This inspired MacDonough to seek a career at sea, and he applied for a midshipman's warrant with the aid of Senator Henry Latimer. This was granted on February 5, 1800. Around this time, for unknown reasons, the 16 year old changed the spelling of his last name from McDonough to MacDonough. Once he left the family homestead, he never returned.

**Page 65 Cannonball in Lewes Wall** After the October 1812 naval engagement in which the US warship *Wasp,* commanded by Capt. Jacob Jones of Delaware, captured the British *Frolic,* the Delaware Bay was blockaded by part of the British fleet under Commodore Sir John Beresford. At Lewes, Colonel Samuel B. Davis refused Britain's demands for ship supplies. On April 5 and 6, 1813 naval vessels led by *HMS Poictiers* briefly and ineffectually bombarded the town. Numerous homes and businesses were damaged. This structure, the McCracken family home, still bears visible traces of the engagement, including an iron cannonball that is lodged in its foundation. (Courtesy Lewes Maritime Museum)

**Page 65 Pea Patch Island** As early as 1794, the architect Pierre-Charles L'Enfant recommended a fort on this muddy island to protect Philadelphia from attack.

The War of 1812 confirmed that forts needed to lie at a considerable distance from the cities they defended, and Pea Patch Island, though at the time a marshy unstable mass, became a fort candidate for protecting Philadelphia and Wilmington, despite these drawbacks. Delaware didn't have sufficient resources to build a fort there, and so its legislature ceded the island to the Federal government in 1813 for that purpose. The Federal government, however, did nothing immediate about fort construction.

A group of alarmed Philadelphians, worried that Delaware Bay was not sufficiently protected against the British, organized a Committee of Defense in August 1814, chaired by Thomas McKean, former Pennsylvania governor. The committee coordinated efforts with the Delaware and New Jersey governors and leading Wilmington citizens to bear down on Washington officials to move forward. They communicated with the Secretaries of the War and Navy Departments, requesting a battery of 32 twenty-four pounders on Pea Patch Island and fortifications on the New Jersey side at Red Bank and Newbold's Point.

The Navy Department approved these and additional batteries at Fort Mifflin. All these forts were financed not by Federal monies, but by Delaware, Pennsylvania, and New Jersey state efforts. The Bank of Pennsylvania alone advanced $300,000.

This upper Delaware Bay regional plan of defense was largely coordinated by Capt. Samuel Babcock who was working nearby on similar defenses in Philadelphia. During this time, a seawall and dykes were built around the island. There is no known evidence that any progress was made on the actual fortification by the end of the War of 1812.

Construction of a traditional star shaped fort on Pea Patch Island finally began sometime before Dec. 8, 1817. Completion of the project was delayed years past the proposed date due to uneven settling, improper pile placement and the island's marshy nature. By 1824, a serviceable fort was in place. Fort Delaware's first documented commander was Maj. Alexander C.W. Fanning, who took command sometime before 1825. (map: Army Corps of Engineers files, National Archives, Philadelphia Branch)

**Page 66 Chesapeake Bay Orientations** Between 1607 and 1609, John Smith was the first English explorer to map the Chesapeake Bay area. Smith encountered Delaware's Nanticoke Native American tribe, which he referred to as the Kuskarawaock or Cuskarawaock, near the confluence of the Nanticoke River and Broad Creek.

Maryland records from 1696 suggest the Nanticoke had 10 towns, and they doubtless had small villages on Nanticoke tributaries that John Smith did not see. There were about 600 American Indians living on the

Nanticoke River in the early 17th century. The word "Nanticoke" derives from Algonquian words meaning 'Tidewater people' or 'They who ply the tidewater stream.'

The original European settlers in the area were Marylanders who had moved up the Nanticoke River drainage in search of inexpensive land on which to establish farms, shipping/trading points, mills, and shipyards. Almost none of the land was divided into large estates; the creation of large landed plantations was not a pattern in this area.

The land that became Laurel is sited on Broad Creek. Barkley Townsend purchased land there in 1789, laid out Laurel's town lots on its south side, and began to sell them. Laurel sat on land that had originally been an Indian reservation established in 1711 by the State of Maryland. At that time, all of the land in western and southern Delaware was considered by Lord Baltimore - though not William Penn! - to be in Maryland. The reservation existed until 1740.

Seaford, 6 miles north of Laurel, grew up around the area adjacent to the main furnace for Deep Creek Iron Works at the confluence of Deep Creek and the Nanticoke River.

The furnace, one of the oldest blast furnaces for processing bog iron into wrought iron in what is now southern Delaware, was established by Jonathan Vaughn. He came from Chester, PA and began acquiring land for it circa 1763. Deep Creek's forge for processing its pig iron was 4 miles northeast at present day Middleford.

The Revolutionary War interrupted Vaughn's business, and he never resumed involvement with it, though grist and saw-mills owned by the company (and a distillery on their property) continued to operate.

The 7,000 acres held by Deep Creek Iron Works were broken up among various founders' heirs by legislative act in 1802 and again in 1805. The present Hearn Mill, shown in the photo here, was the last operating grist mill in lower Delaware, an indirect descendent of a grist mill which had been owned by Deep Creek Iron Works in its heyday.

**Page 67 Bishop Peter Spencer** Born a slave, Bishop Spencer was the father of Delaware's independent Black church movement. In 1813, he founded the Union Church of Africans, presently known as the African Union Methodist Protestant Church. The mother AUMP church stood on what is today Peter Spencer Plaza in Wilmington from 1813 to 1970. The Union American Methodist Episcopal Church (UAME), formally organized in 1865, traces its origins to Spencer. He was also the founder of "August Quarterly" in 1813, one of the oldest Black folk festivals in America.

**Page 68 Old Stone Tavern, Little Creek** The settlement of Little Creek grew up at a wharf on the line between neighboring plantations. Elijah McDowell built a store in town and dealt largely in grain, brought in from the surrounding country and shipped by Manolve Hayes, Sr., a prosperous farmer and politician who operated a steamship line to Philadelphia.

This Old Stone Tavern was never a tavern but rather a house, built in 1822 by Hayes and his wife's cousin, John Bell. Hayes also built the nearby Octagonal Schoolhouse (1830–1831). The so-called tavern is of gneiss rich in muscovite. Hayes probably brought the stone by boat from Chester County, Pennsylvania, or possibly from Maryland. A tax assessment of 1828 for Little Creek Hundred demonstrates the uniqueness of these stone buildings: there were ninety-seven local structures of frame, sixty of log, twenty-seven of brick, and only two of stone. After the railroad was built the place lost its shipping trade and declined economically.

**Page 69 Scene of Wheat, Scene of Corn** Caesar Rodney's young brother, Thomas, described the life of the mid-eighteenth century farmer in Kent County as "very simple, plain, and social. The largest farmers did not sow over twenty acres of wheat, nor tend more than thirty acres of Indian corn, and there was very few of this sort, so that all the families in the county had a great deal of idle time." But the French and Indian War caused a rise in prices, produce became more valuable, and "in a few years the country became engaged in more pursuits and put on quite a new appearance."

In the last quarter of the 17th century Philadelphia began to dominate the region's economic scene. Farmers in all three Delaware counties sent their grains to the local milling centers, where wheat and corn were then shipped to Philadelphia for export to the West Indies, other North American colonies, and southern European countries. Most Delaware farmers by the early 19th century were within a half-day's journey of a mill or shipping wharf. The grain scale shown here, also known as a corn balance or chondrometer, was used for measuring the volume and weight of grain. The grain merchant sent a sample of the grain through the funnel into the small brass bucket and measured the two variables. The outcome would determine price and space required to store the crop in question.

This scale was used in Dayett Mill, Newark. Donated by Ray Johnson (last owner of the mill) to the Pencader Heritage Museum before the property was sold to the State of Delaware.

**Page 70 The Vesta Steamboat** This ship model from Wilmington artist Frank E. Schoonover may or may not be *The Vesta*. He doesn't label it, and we don't have ship's plans for the boat. However, we can guess that *The Vesta* probably looked something like this. Why? Because it took a while before mariners gained sufficient confidence with steam-propelled vessels, most of the initial steam craft were also outfitted with a sail rig, as in the case of this model.

*The Vesta* was co-owned by the Warner brothers and George Coxen, captain of the ship. Initially named *The Vestal*, the ship's name changed in 1815. The Wilmington-Philadelphia trip originally required 8 hours at a fare of $1.00. Her first arrival in Wilmington caused much enthusiasm; people turned out in large numbers to visit the steamboat.

Seven steamboats were reported to be operating on the Delaware River in 1813. Steamboats were gradually used with increasing frequency. In 1819, *The Vesta* was the first steamboat to venture down Delaware Bay from Philadelphia to Cape May, NJ. It completed the trip twice a week. [Three masted ship model on white backdrop, 1906, 2017239_25_017, Frank E. Schoonover negatives (Accession 2017.239), Hagley Museum & Library, Wilmington, DE 19807]

**Page 70 Easternmost Lock of C&D Canal, Delaware City** Although the idea of a waterway crossing the upper Delmarva peninsula was suggested in the 1600s, the canal didn't become a reality until 1829. Private investors, operating as the Chesapeake and Delaware Canal Company, raised the money to build the canal by selling stock. The canal cost $2,250,000 and took five years to build. Over 2,600 workers, including many Irish immigrant and African American laborers, dug the canal with picks and shovels for wages of 75¢ a day, paid in scrip.

When they were done, they had created a 14-mile long ditch that was ten feet deep and sixty feet wide, with four locks to carry ships over high and low waters, shortening the water route between Philadelphia and Baltimore by more than 300 miles. The canal opened on October 17, 1829 with great celebrations. All manner of crafts used it. Initially, horse and mule drawn barges predominated, but eventually steam-powered vessels made up the majority of canal traffic.

Shown in the photo here is the original easternmost lock in Delaware City. This lock and the lock at St. Georges each had a lift of 6 to 8 feet, and in the two locks at Chesapeake City, the lift was 14 to 16 feet. Originally, each lock was 100 feet long, 22 feet wide, and 10 feet deep. This branch of the canal connects with the main C&D Canal two miles inland. The modern day Delaware River entrance is two miles south. In 1927, the Army Corps of Engineers dredged the waterway into a sea-level passage, eliminating the need for locks.

**Page 71 Lafayette Tours the States** The Marquis de Lafayette, on a visit to Delaware in 1824, wrote in a young girl's album: "After having seen nearly half a century ago, the banks of the Brandywine a scene of bloody fighting, I am happy now to find upon them the seat of industry, beauty and mutual friendship." During the battle, he had been shot through the leg after he had leaped from his horse, yet still maintained furious sword battle with the British. This won the undying respect of the American troops.

**Page 72 Colonial Hearths** As to the Hendrickson House: There was once a woodshed just outside the window. Firewood could be passed through the window without having to carry it around the house. The window ledge is deep, so it could hold wood and also let it dry in the window if it was wet or green.

More typically in this era, such an opening would have been where the beehive oven would have been. In Delaware, as in the other colonies that later became the United States, most households had a beehive oven (a design that had been around since the Middle Ages).

The oven itself would have been built against the outer wall, to prevent home interiors from overheating in summertime, as bread needed to be baked once a week, regardless of season. You can see the arrangement clearly from the back end of the beehive ovens at the Wilson-Warner House (upper right).

The fireplace spot in the Hale Byrnes House (upper left) where the beehive oven originally was has been bricked over. When this home was built in 1750, the new dutch oven was already well along in replacing the beehive. The Dutch, since at least the late 1600s, had been commercially using a sand casting technique for brass known since Italian metallurgist Vannoccio Biringuccio first explained it in 1540. They called the resulting pot, simply, a breadpan. Englishman Abraham Darby studied the process, then patented his own "Dutch Oven," instead using cast iron, in 1707. The new oven heated more evenly and was easier to work with than the clumsy beehive design.

The Dutch House in New Castle today has a cast-iron dutch oven sitting prominently in front of its kitchen fireplace (lower left). However, this fireplace is a Federal-style model from an 1823 kitchen makeover. The 1657 house most likely was built too early, and was too rustic, to be using the new brass ovens. Because the original house's fireplaces would have been small, it's probable the bread baking was done in a separate out-building during that early period. (Hendrickson hearth courtesy Old Swedes Foundation; Hale Byrnes hearth courtesy Delaware Society for the Preservation of Antiquities; Dutch House hearth courtesy New Castle Historical Society; Wilson-Warner hearth courtesy Historic Odessa Foundation, Inc.)

**Page 73 Octagonal Schoolhouse, Little Creek** This district #12 schoolhouse was originally called Pleasant Hill Academy. It had 87 students when it opened and was, in its time, one of the finest schools in Kent County. Two circles of desks were set up inside: the outer circle of boys faced the wall; the inner circle of girls faced the center.

As early as 1792, Delaware's constitutional convention had called for the establishment of free public schools by legislative act. The State school fund was established in 1796, and, after 1817, State aid was available for the education of poor children.

Willard Hall, a Harvard trained lawyer who served in Delaware's General Assembly, US Congress and almost half-a-century as a federal judge, was responsible for drawing up plans for the state's 133 school districts.

www.ingramcontent.com/pod-product-compliance
Lightning Source LLC
Chambersburg PA
CBHW041616120626
46551CB00003B/467